Gerard Manley Hopkins

The Works of
Gerard Manley Hopkins

❦

with an Introduction and Bibliography

The Wordsworth Poetry Library

This edition published 1994 by Wordsworth Editions Ltd,
Cumberland House, Crib Street, Ware, Hertfordshire SG12 9ET.

ISBN 1-85326-413-X

Printed and bound in Denmark by Nørhaven.

The paper in this book is produced from pure wood
pulp, without the use of chlorine or any other substance
harmful to the environment. The energy used in its
production consists almost entirely of hydroelectricity
and heat generated from waste materials, thereby
conserving fossil fuels and contributing little to the
greenhouse effect.

CONTENTS

CONTENTS

INTRODUCTION

PARADOXICALLY, Gerard Manley Hopkins, whose poetry
was regarded as inaccessible and 'modern' long after his
death, was in many ways a characteristic Victorian. Born
in 1844, to prosperous and cultivated middle-class
parents, he was to be much influenced by Ruskin, whose
minuteness of observation Hopkins emulated, both in his
drawings and in much of his later verse. His education
at Highgate School had the traditional grounding in the
classics. While he demonstrated his singularity by
successfully wagering that he could go without drinking
anything for three weeks, and in being threatened with
expulsion for some trifling obstinacy, he also won a prize
for a long and erudite poem. Arrived at Balliol College,
Oxford, he continued to write poetry as well as having a
busy and companiable social life. Although touchy and
sometimes arrogant, he had great sweetness, and was
loved by many, among them the future Poet Laureate,
Robert Bridges, whose patient advocacy of Hopkins's
poetry eventually secured its reputation.

Oxford was seething with theological debate. Many of
the devout, fearing rational agnosticism and repelled by
the fervid, populist Protestantism which had followed
Wesley's religious revival, were attracted by the beauty
and mystery of Roman Catholic rituals and traditions; the

Anglo-Catholicism pioneered by Keble naturally appealed to the thoughtful, sensitive and 'aesthetic' young. However, the English still regarded the Roman church with fascinated horror, and the defection to Rome of prominent Anglo-Catholics like Manning and Newman caused real fear and outrage. It can be seen that Hopkins's conversion to the Roman Catholic church – undertaken with characteristic scruples and self-examination – was an aspect of his Victorian temper. Although his parents accepted this with surprising equanimity, Hopkins assumed their hostility. He had visited Newman in Birmingham just before his conversion and, on leaving Oxford, went to teach in Newman's Oratory school while he pondered his vocation. In 1868 he entered the Jesuit Novitiate at Manresa House, Roehampton. Hopkins's choice of the Society of Jesus (formed as the spiritual army of the church, and bound by the demanding Spiritual Exercises of its founder, St Ignatius Loyola – and traditionally distrusted by the British) mark his desire for its rigorous discipline with its emphasis on soldierly obedience. All his life he was to dwell on his own faults with painful piety, and his early journals describe torments of remorse for faults which even his confessors regarded as nugatory.

He burnt all his poems when he decided on the priesthood (though Bridges had copies of many of them), having decided that the two vocations were incompatible, and now embarked on the protracted Jesuit novitiate at Roehampton and Stonyhurst in Lancashire. In the summer of 1874 his superiors, anxious about his health and spirits, sent him to the Society's house in St Bueno's, Wales. This was a comparatively happy period in what was largely an unhappy life. He liked the Welsh and set about learning their language; and he loved the countryside, especially a famous holy place, St Winifred's Well.

In 1875 the wreck of the German ship, the *Deutschland*, which was carrying five exiled nuns, inspired his great ode. Although he had been encouraged in this by a superior it was never published in his lifetime, and even the faithful Bridges found it impenetrable. But patient reading reveals its passion, beauty and strength. Modern atheists or agnostics should try to sympathize with Hopkins's passionate religious feelings and his sense of loss when they failed him. For him, the love of God, and rejoicing delight in the natural world which 'spoke' God's greatness, were emotions far stronger than earthly love, and were expressed with a lover's intensity.

Hopkins's 'sprung rhythm', his way of scanning much of his verse by stressing (or bouncing on) only those words which carry emotional weight, and letting the remaining syllables scramble in anyhow, is daunting on first encounter, and rendered even more daunting to the new reader by his own Preface. The best way, and the way he himself recommends, is to read the poems aloud, stressing the syllables he accents and speaking the others rapidly and lightly. For instance, '*Spring and Fall*' reads at first as if it runs '*Mar*garet, are you *griev*ing/Over *Gold*engrove un*leav*ing?' – lines with two stresses each. But his accent on the last syllable of 'Margaret' indicates that they should be read as having four stresses:

'*Margaret, are* you *griev*ing/O*ve*r *Gold*engrove un*leav*-ing?' – and the rest of the poem now reads much more gratefully. Only the Hopkins expert can read poems like '*Harry Ploughman*' easily, but '*The Wreck of the Deutsch-land*' soon yields its powerful and flexible rhythms, in which the same stanza-form can accommodate both the rhapsodic '*Is out* with it! *Oh*,/We *lash* with the *best* or *worst*/Word *last*. How a *lush*-kept *plush*-capped sloe . . .' and the funeral march of

> 'Some *find* me a *sword*; *some*
> The *flange* and the *rail*; *flame*,
> *Fang*, or *flood*' goes *Death* on *drum* . . .

This great poem, with its vibrant meditations on the relation of humankind to God, and on the Passion of Christ echoed on the suffering of the nuns, led to many more poems, as his long-frustrated creativity broke forth. The Sensuous and accessible sonnets, '*God's Grandeur*', '*The Starlight Night*' and '*Spring*' were written in 1877, and show his preoccupation with what he called 'inscape' and 'instress'. 'Inscape' is, broadly speaking, the indi-vidual and characteristic form which characterizes the God-given uniqueness of a particular object or landscape, while 'instress' is the intrinsic power stemming from the divine, which sustains and encompasses it, as well as providing the communication between the observer and what is observed. These stem from the writing of Walter Pater, and from Hopkins's reading of Duns Scotus, a Scottish theologian of the medieval Church, whose emphasis on the 'thisness' [*haeccitas*] of the created world lies in contradiction to the Jesuits' 'official' theologian,

Thomas Aquinas.

Inscape and instress are perfectly exemplified in the great sonnet, '*The Windhover*', where Hopkins uses his sprung rhythm in the classic sonnet form – fourteen lines, each with five stresses, divided into the eight-line octave and the six-line sestet. The octave evokes the falcon in chivalric terms, and goes on to echo its motion, 'in his riding/Of the rolling level underneath him steady air, and striding/High there, how he rung on the rein of a wimpling wing . . .' The sestet conflates the falcon with Christ as heroic saviour:

> Brute beauty and valour and act, oh air, pride, plume, here
> Buckle! AND the fire that breaks from thee then, a
>   billion
> Times told lovelier, more dangerous, O my chevalier!

As so often with Hopkins's idiosyncratic use of words, 'buckle' can be read in various ways. It may be the buckling together of the windhover's attributes, leading to the idea of a knight or chevalier buckling on armour. It can carry the idea of 'buckling-to', engaging the adversary. Or it may mean collapsing together, as in buckled metal which flashes out light, leading towards the way the 'blue-streak embers . . . gash gold-vermilion'.

In 1878, after some teaching at Chesterfield, Hopkins returned to Stonyhurst whose bleakness seems to have inhibited his writing, though he produced '*The Loss of the Euridice*', a shipwreck poem far more Victorian in atmosphere than '*Deutschland*', and the gentle and pious '*May Magnificat*'. He suffered horribly from the mockery his eccentricities inspired: an inept journeyman

sermon produced gales of discomfiting laughter from his
fellow novices. In December 1879 he was sent to Oxford,
where his poetic powers revived. Here, along with the
sentimental but heartfelt '*Bugler's First Communion*', we
find a growing preoccupation with the transience of
beauty, so easily despoiled. In '*Duns Scotus's Oxford*' the
'Towery city and branchy between towers;/Cuckoo-
echoing, bell-swarmed, lark-charmed, rook-racked,
river-rounded' is disfigured by 'a base and brickish skirt'.
'*Binsey Poplars*', with ineffable lightness and grace,
addresses the same theme:

> My aspens dear, whose airy cages quelled,
> Quelled or quenched in leaves the leaping sun,
> Are felled, felled, are all felled . . .
> O if we but knew what we do
>   When we delve or hew –
> Hack and wrack the growing green!
>   Since country is so tender
> To touch, her being so slender,
> That, like this sleek and seeing ball
> But a prick will make no eye at all . . .

Always peoccupied with perception, he gives another
unforgettable optical image in '*The Candle Indoors*' whose
'to-fro tender trambeans truckle at the eye'.

The note of elegy for transient nature still sounds in
'*Inversnaid*', written on a Scottish holiday in 1881. This
was soon followed by '*Spring and Fall*' whose limpid
wistfulness associated with childhood innocence is Victo-
rian in flavour. Hopkins nevertheless adds his own
unmistakeable instress:

Ah! as the heart grows older
It will come to such sights colder
By and by, nor spare a sigh
Though worlds of wanwood leafmeal lie.

Back at Stonyhurst, he wrote 'The Leaden Echo and the
Golden Echo' (choruses from an uncompleted poetic
drama about St Winifred's Well) in which sorrow for the
transience of earthly beauty is answered by confidence in
God, 'beauty's self and beauty's giver'. But now the most
desolate period of his life was upon him. In 1884 the
Society moved him to Dublin to teach classics at the newly
formed Catholic university: 'To seem the stranger lies my
lot', he laments, and what mystics call 'the dark night of
the soul' pervades the 'terrible sonnets' which he wrote
during this time. The mood of black horror which
informs the spiky and apocalyptic 'Spelt from Sibyl's
Leaves' is turned in on himself:

I am gall, I am heartburn. God's most deep decree
Bitter would have me taste: my taste was me.

There is another of Hopkins's multiple meanings in 'I
wake to feel the fell of dark, not day'. 'Fell', assonant with
'feel' (and 'felt') has as its primary meaning the old word
for the furred skin, or pelt, of an animal. But we are
required to hold in our minds the adjective 'fell',
('dreadful' or 'fearful'), the past tense of the verb 'to fall'
and, possibly, the sense of 'fell' as 'mountain'. 'No worst,
there is none' echoes Shakespeare's darkest play, King
Lear:

O the mind, mind has mountains; cliffs of fall
Frightful, sheer, no-man-fathomed. Hold them cheap
May who ne'er hung there . . .

while feelings of frustration and impotence are evident in
'*Thou art indeed just lord*' ('Time's eunuch') and 'To R.B.'
In the sonnet to St Alphonsus Rodriguez, chivalric echoes
from '*The Windhover*' –

> 'Honour is flashed off exploit, so we say;
> And those strokes once that gashed flesh or galled
>   shield . . .
> Should tongue that time now . . .

are contrasted with the kind of prosaic, quotidian
martyrdom which Hopkins felt he was enduring, 'those
years and years by of world without event', unrecognised
and unrewarded:

> But be the war within, the brand we wield
> Unseen, the heroic breast not outward-steeled
> Earth hears no hurtle then from fiercest fray.

It was bitter for him that the Jesuits, who so often kept
their spiritual warriors on the move, left him in Dublin,
harrassed and exhausted until his death from typhoid in
June 1889. The Society had done its best for him by its
lights but this sensitive, over-scrupulous and unusual man
had been formed with too little capacity for human
happiness.

FURTHER READING

Catherine Phillips (ed.), *Gerard Manley Hopkins* (the poems, with selections from the letters and journals), Oxford, 1986.

Humphrey House and Graham Storey (ed.), *The Journal and Papers of Gerard Manley Hopkins*, London, 1959.

Norman White, *Hopkins: A Literary Biography*, Oxford, 1992.

Robert Bernard Martin, *Gerard Manley Hopkins: A Very Private Life*, London, 1991.

Poems of
GERARD MANLEY
HOPKINS

CATHARINAE

HVNC LIBRVM

QVI FILII EIVS CARISSIMI

POETAE DEBITAM INGENIO LAVDEM EXPECTANTIS

SERVM TAMEN MONVMENTVM ESSET

ANNVM AETATIS XCVIII AGENTI

VETERIS AMICITIAE PIGNVS

D D D

R B

Our generation already is overpast,
And thy lov'd legacy, Gerard, hath lain
Coy in my home ; as once thy heart was fain
Of shelter, when God's terror held thee fast
In life's wild wood at Beauty and Sorrow aghast ;
Thy sainted sense trammel'd in ghostly pain,
Thy rare ill-broker'd talent in disdain :
Yet love of Christ will win man's love at last.

  Hell wars without ; but, dear, the while my hands
Gather'd thy book, I heard, this wintry day,
Thy spirit thank me, in his young delight
Stepping again upon the yellow sands.
  Go forth : amidst our chaffinch flock display
Thy plumage of far wonder and heavenward flight !

                   Chilswell, Jan. 1918.

AUTHOR'S PREFACE

THE poems in this book are written some in Running Rhythm, the common rhythm in English use, some in Sprung Rhythm, and some in a mixture of the two. And those in the common rhythm are some counter-pointed, some not.

Common English rhythm, called Running Rhythm above, is measured by feet of either two or three syllables and (putting aside the imperfect feet at the beginning and end of lines and also some unusual measures, in which feet seem to be paired together and double or composite feet to arise) never more or less.

Every foot has one principal stress or accent, and this or the syllable it falls on may be called the Stress of the foot and the other part, the one or two unaccented syllables, the Slack. Feet (and the rhythms made out of them) in which the stress comes first are called Falling Feet and Falling Rhythms, feet and rhythm in which the slack comes first are called Rising Feet and Rhythms, and if the stress is between two slacks there will be Rocking Feet and Rhythms. These distinctions are real and true to nature; but for purposes of scanning it is a great convenience to follow the example of music

and take the stress always first, as the accent or the
chief accent always comes first in a musical bar. If this
is done there will be in common English verse only two
possible feet—the so-called accentual Trochee and
Dactyl, and correspondingly only two possible uniform
rhythms, the so-called Trochaic and Dactylic. But
they may be mixed and then what the Greeks called a
Logaoedic Rhythm arises. These are the facts and
according to these the scanning of ordinary regularly-
written English verse is very simple indeed and to bring
in other principles is here unnecessary.

But because verse written strictly in these feet and
by these principles will become same and tame the
poets have brought in licences and departures from rule
to give variety, and especially when the natural rhythm
is rising, as in the common ten-syllable or five-foot
verse, rhymed or blank. These irregularities are chiefly
Reversed Feet and Reversed or Counterpoint Rhythm,
which two things are two steps or degrees of licence in
the same kind. By a reversed foot I mean the putting
the stress where, to judge by the rest of the measure,
the slack should be and the slack where the stress, and
this is done freely at the beginning of a line and, in the
course of a line, after a pause; only scarcely ever in the
second foot or place and never in the last, unless when
the poet designs some extraordinary effect; for these
places are characteristic and sensitive and cannot well be
touched. But the reversal of the first foot and of some
middle foot after a strong pause is a thing so natural
that our poets have generally done it, from Chaucer

down, without remark and it commonly passes unnoticed and cannot be said to amount to a formal change of rhythm, but rather is that irregularity which all natural growth and motion shews. If however the reversal is repeated in two feet running, especially so as to include the sensitive second foot, it must be due either to great want of ear or else is a calculated effect, the super-inducing or *mounting* of a new rhythm upon the old; and since the new or mounted rhythm is actually heard and at the same time the mind naturally supplies the natural or standard foregoing rhythm, for we do not forget what the rhythm is that by rights we should be hearing, two rhythms are in some manner running at once and we have something answerable to counter-point in music, which is two or more strains of tune going on together, and this is Counterpoint Rhythm. Of this kind of verse Milton is the great master and the choruses of *Samson Agonistes* are written throughout in it—but with the disadvantage that he does not let the reader clearly know what the ground-rhythm is meant to be and so they have struck most readers as merely irregular. And in fact if you counterpoint throughout, since one only of the counter rhythms is actually heard, the other is really destroyed or cannot come to exist, and what is written is one rhythm only and probably Sprung Rhythm, of which I now speak.

Sprung Rhythm, as used in this book, is measured by feet of from one to four syllables, regularly, and for particular effects any number of weak or slack syllables may be used. It has one stress, which falls on the only syllable, if there is only one, or, if there are more, then scanning as above, on the first, and so gives rise to four sorts of feet, a monosyllable and the so-called accentual Trochee, Dactyl, and the First Paeon. And there will be four corresponding natural rhythms ; but nominally the feet are mixed and any one may follow any other. And hence Sprung Rhythm differs from Running Rhythm in having or being only one nominal rhythm, a mixed or 'logaoedic' one, instead of three, but on the other hand in having twice the flexibility of foot, so that any two stresses may either follow one another running or be divided by one, two, or three slack syllables. But strict Sprung Rhythm cannot be counterpointed. In Sprung Rhythm, as in logaoedic rhythm generally, the feet are assumed to be equally long or strong and their seeming inequality is made up by pause or stressing.

Remark also that it is natural in Sprung Rhythm for the lines to be *rove over*, that is for the scanning of each line immediately to take up that of the one before, so that if the first has one or more syllables at its end the other must have so many the less at its beginning ; and in fact the scanning runs on without break from the beginning, say, of a stanza to the end and all the stanza is one long strain, though written in lines asunder.

Two licences are natural to Sprung Rhythm. The one is rests, as in music ; but of this an example is scarcely to be found in this book, unless in the *Echos*, second line. The other is *hangers* or *outrides*, that is one, two, or three slack syllables added to a foot and not counting in the nominal scanning. They are so called because they seem to hang below the line or ride forward or backward from it in another dimension than the line itself, according to a principle needless to explain here. These outriding half feet or hangers are marked by a loop underneath them, and plenty of them will be found.

The other marks are easily understood, namely accents, where the reader might be in doubt which syllable should have the stress; slurs, that is loops *over* syllables, to tie them together into the time of one; little loops at the end of a line to shew that the rhyme goes on to the first letter of the next line; what in music are called pauses ⌢, to shew that the syllable should be dwelt on; and twirls ∼, to mark reversed or counterpointed rhythm.

Note on the nature and history of Sprung Rhythm— Sprung Rhythm is the most natural of things. For (1) it is the rhythm of common speech and of written prose, when rhythm is perceived in them. (2) It is the rhythm of all but the most monotonously regular music, so that in the words of choruses and refrains and in songs written closely to music it arises. (3) It is found in nursery rhymes, weather saws, and so on; because, however these may have been once made in running rhythm, the terminations having dropped off by the change of language, the stresses come together and so the rhythm is sprung. (4) It arises in common verse when reversed or counterpointed, for the same reason.

But nevertheless in spite of all this and though Greek

and Latin lyric verse, which is well known, and the old English verse seen in *Pierce Ploughman* are in sprung rhythm, it has in fact ceased to be used since the Elizabethan age, Greene being the last writer who can be said to have recognised it. For perhaps there was not, down to our days, a single, even short, poem in English in which sprung rhythm is employed—not for single effects or in fixed places—but as the governing principle of the scansion. I say this because the contrary has been asserted : if it is otherwise the poem should be cited.

———————

Some of the sonnets in this book[1] are in five-foot, some in six-foot or Alexandrine lines.

Nos. 13 and 22 are Curtal-Sonnets, that is they are constructed in proportions resembling those of the sonnet proper, namely $6 + 4$ instead of $8 + 6$, with however a halfline tailpiece (so that the equation is rather $\frac{12}{2} + \frac{9}{2} = \frac{21}{2} = 10\frac{1}{2}$).

[1] See previous note.

EARLY POEMS

For a Picture of
St. Dorothea

I BEAR a basket lined with grass;
I am so light, I am so fair,
That men must wonder as I pass
And at the basket that I bear,
Where in a newly-drawn green litter
Sweet flowers I carry,—sweets for bitter.

Lilies I shew you, lilies none,
None in Caesar's gardens blow,—
And a quince in hand,—not one
Is set upon your boughs below;
Not set, because their buds not spring;
Spring not, 'cause world is wintering.

But these were found in the East and South
Where Winter is the clime forgot.—
The dewdrop on the larkspur's mouth
O should it then be quenchèd not?
In starry water-meads they drew
These drops: which be they? stars or dew?

Had she a quince in hand? Yet gaze:
Rather it is the sizing moon.
Lo, linkèd heavens with milky ways!
That was her larkspur row.—So soon?
Sphered so fast, sweet soul?—We see
Nor fruit, nor flowers, nor Dorothy.

2

Heaven-Haven

A nun takes the veil

I HAVE desired to go
    Where springs not fail,
To fields where flies no sharp and sided hail
    And a few lilies blow.

And I have asked to be
    Where no storms come,
Where the green swell is in the havens dumb,
    And out of the swing of the sea.

3

The Habit of Perfection

ELECTED Silence, sing to me
And beat upon my whorlèd ear,
Pipe me to pastures still and be
The music that I care to hear.

Shape nothing, lips; be lovely-dumb:
It is the shut, the curfew sent
From there where all surrenders come
Which only makes you eloquent.

Be shellèd, eyes, with double dark
And find the uncreated light:
This ruck and reel which you remark
Coils, keeps, and teases simple sight.

Palate, the hutch of tasty lust,
Desire not to be rinsed with wine:
The can must be so sweet, the crust
So fresh that come in fasts divine!

Nostrils, your careless breath that spend
Upon the stir and keep of pride,
What relish shall the censers send
Along the sanctuary side!

O feel-of-primrose hands, O feet
That want the yield of plushy sward,
But you shall walk the golden street
And you unhouse and house the Lord.

And, Poverty, be thou the bride
And now the marriage feast begun,
And lily-coloured clothes provide
Your spouse not laboured-at nor spun.

POEMS 1876–1889

THE WRECK
OF THE DEUTSCHLAND

*To the
happy memory of five Franciscan Nuns
exiles by the Falk Laws
drowned between midnight and morning of
Dec. 7th, 1875*

PART THE FIRST

I

Thou mastering me
God! giver of breath and bread;
World's strand, sway of the sea;
Lord of living and dead;
Thou hast bound bones and veins in me, fastened me flesh,
And after it almost unmade, what with dread,
Thy doing: and dost thou touch me afresh?
Over again I feel thy finger and find thee.

2

I did say yes
O at lightning and lashed rod ;
Thou heardst me truer than tongue confess
Thy terror, O Christ, O God ;
Thou knowest the walls, altar and hour and night :
The swoon of a heart that the sweep and the hurl of thee trod
Hard down with a horror of height :
And the midriff astrain with leaning of, laced with fire of stress.

3

The frown of his face
Before me, the hurtle of hell
Behind, where, where was a, where was a place ?
I whirled out wings that spell
And fled with a fling of the heart to the heart of the Host.
My heart, but you were dovewinged, I can tell,
Carrier-witted, I am bold to boast,
To flash from the flame to the flame then, tower from the grace
to the grace.

4

I am soft sift
In an hourglass—at the wall
Fast, but mined with a motion, a drift,
And it crowds and it combs to the fall ;
I steady as a water in a well, to a poise, to a pane,
But roped with, always, all the way down from the tall
Fells or flanks of the voel, a vein
Of the gospel proffer, a pressure, a principle, Christ's gift.

5

I kiss my hand
To the stars, lovely-asunder
Starlight, wafting him out of it; and
Glow, glory in thunder;
Kiss my hand to the dappled-with-damson west:
Since, tho' he is under the world's splendour and wonder,
His mystery must be instressed, stressed;
For I greet him the days I meet him, and bless when I understand.

6

Not out of his bliss
Springs the stress felt
Nor first from heaven (and few know this)
Swings the stroke dealt—
Stroke and a stress that stars and storms deliver,
That guilt is hushed by, hearts are flushed by and melt—
But it rides time like riding a river
(And here the faithful waver, the faithless fable and miss).

7

It dates from day
Of his going in Galilee;
Warm-laid grave of a womb-life grey;
Manger, maiden's knee;
The dense and the driven Passion, and frightful sweat;
Thence the discharge of it, there its swelling to be,
Though felt before, though in high flood yet—
What none would have known of it, only the heart, being hard at bay,

8

Is out with it! Oh,
We lash with the best or worst
Word last!   How a lush-kept plush-capped sloe
Will, mouthed to flesh-burst,
Gush!—flush the man, the being with it, sour or sweet,
Brim, in a flash, full!—Hither then, last or first,
To hero of Calvary, Christ,'s feet—
Never ask if meaning it, wanting it, warned of it—men go.

9

Be adored among men,
God, three-numberèd form;
Wring thy rebel, dogged in den,
Man's malice, with wrecking and storm.
Beyond saying sweet, past telling of tongue,
Thou art lightning and love, I found it, a winter and warm;
Father and fondler of heart thou hast wrung:
Hast thy dark descending and most art merciful then.

10

With an anvil-ding
And with fire in him forge thy will
Or rather, rather then, stealing as Spring
Through him, melt him but master him still:
Whether at once, as once at a crash Paul,
Or as Austin, a lingering-out sweet skill,
Make mercy in all of us, out of us all
Mastery, but be adored, but be adored King.

PART THE SECOND

11

'Some find me a sword; some
The flange and the rail; flame,
Fang, or flood' goes Death on drum,
And storms bugle his fame.
But we dream we are rooted in earth—Dust!
Flesh falls within sight of us, we, though our flower the same,
Wave with the meadow, forget that there must
The sour scythe cringe, and the blear share come.

12

On Saturday sailed from Bremen,
American-outward-bound,
Take settler and seamen, tell men with women,
Two hundred souls in the round—
O Father, not under thy feathers nor ever as guessing
The goal was a shoal, of a fourth the doom to be drowned;
Yet did the dark side of the bay of thy blessing
Not vault them, the millions of rounds of thy mercy not reeve
even them in?

13

Into the snows she sweeps,
Hurling the haven behind,
The Deutschland, on Sunday; and so the sky keeps,
For the infinite air is unkind,
And the sea flint-flake, black-backed in the regular blow,
Sitting Eastnortheast, in cursed quarter, the wind;
Wiry and white-fiery and whirlwind-swivellèd snow
Spins to the widow-making unchilding unfathering deeps.

14

She drove in the dark to leeward,
She struck—not a reef or a rock
But the combs of a smother of sand : night drew her
Dead to the Kentish Knock ;
And she beat the bank down with her bows and the ride of
her keel :
The breakers rolled on her beam with ruinous shock ;
And canvas and compass, the whorl and the wheel
Idle for ever to waft her or wind her with, these she endured.

15

Hope had grown grey hairs,
Hope had mourning on,
Trenched with tears, carved with cares,
Hope was twelve hours gone ;
And frightful a nightfall folded rueful a day
Nor rescue, only rocket and lightship, shone,
And lives at last were washing away :
To the shrouds they took,—they shook in the hurling and
horrible airs.

16

One stirred from the rigging to save
The wild woman-kind below,
With a rope's end round the man, handy and brave—
He was pitched to his death at a blow,
For all his dreadnought breast and braids of thew :
They could tell him for hours, dandled the to and fro
Through the cobbled foam-fleece, what could he do
With the burl of the fountains of air, buck and the flood of the wave?

17

They fought with God's cold—
And they could not and fell to the deck
(Crushed them) or water (and drowned them) or rolled
With the sea-romp over the wreck.
Night roared, with the heart-break hearing a heart-broke rabble,
The woman's wailing, the crying of child without check—
Till a lioness arose breasting the babble,
A prophetess towered in the tumult, a virginal tongue told.

18

Ah, touched in your bower of bone
Are you! turned for an exquisite smart,
Have you! make words break from me here all alone,
Do you!—mother of being in me, heart.
O unteachably after evil, but uttering truth,
Why, tears! is it? tears; such a melting, a madrigal start!
Never-eldering revel and river of youth,
What can it be, this glee? the good you have there of your own?

19

Sister, a sister calling
A master, her master and mine!—
And the inboard seas run swirling and hawling;
The rash smart sloggering brine
Blinds her; but she that weather sees one thing, one;
Has one fetch in her: she rears herself to divine
Ears, and the call of the tall nun
To the men in the tops and the tackle rode over the storm's brawling.

20

She was first of a five and came
Of a coifèd sisterhood.
(O Deutschland, double a desperate name!
O world wide of its good!
But Gertrude, lily, and Luther, are two of a town,
Christ's lily and beast of the waste wood:
From life's dawn it is drawn down,
Abel is Cain's brother and breasts they have sucked the same.)

21

Loathed for a love men knew in them,
Banned by the land of their birth,
Rhine refused them.   Thames would ruin them;
Surf, snow, river and earth
Gnashed: but thou art above, thou Orion of light;
Thy unchancelling poising palms were weighing the worth,
Thou martyr-master: in thy sight
Storm flakes were scroll-leaved flowers, lily showers—sweet
heaven was astrew in them.

22

Five! the finding and sake
And cipher of suffering Christ.
Mark, the mark is of man's make
And the word of it Sacrificed.
But he scores it in scarlet himself on his own bespoken,
Before-time-taken, dearest prizèd and priced—
Stigma, signal, cinquefoil token
For lettering of the lamb's fleece, ruddying of the rose-flake.

23

Joy fall to thee, father Francis,
    Drawn to the Life that died;
With the gnarls of the nails in thee, niche of the lance, his
    Lovescape crucified
And seal of his seraph-arrival! and these thy daughters
    And five-livèd and leavèd favour and pride,
        Are sisterly sealed in wild waters,
To bathe in his fall-gold mercies, to breathe in his all-fire glances.

24

Away in the loveable west,
    On a pastoral forehead of Wales,
I was under a roof here, I was at rest,
    And they the prey of the gales;
She to the black-about air, to the breaker, the thickly
    Falling flakes, to the throng that catches and quails
        Was calling 'O Christ, Christ, come quickly':
The cross to her she calls Christ to her, christens her wild-worst
    Best.

25

The majesty! what did she mean?
    Breathe, arch and original Breath.
Is it love in her of the being as her lover had been?
    Breathe, body of lovely Death.
They were else-minded then, altogether, the men
Woke thee with a *we are perishing* in the weather of Gennesa-
    reth.
        Or is it that she cried for the crown then,
The keener to come at the comfort for feeling the combating keen?

26

For how to the heart's cheering
The down-dugged ground-hugged grey
Hovers off, the jay-blue heavens appearing
Of pied and peeled May!
Blue-beating and hoary-glow height; or night, still higher,
With belled fire and the moth-soft Milky Way,
What by your measure is the heaven of desire,
The treasure never eyesight got, nor was ever guessed what for
the hearing?

27

No, but it was not these.
The jading and jar of the cart,
Time's tasking, it is fathers that asking for ease
Of the sodden-with-its-sorrowing heart,
Not danger, electrical horror; then further it finds
The appealing of the Passion is tenderer in prayer apart:
Other, I gather, in measure her mind's
Burden, in wind's burly and beat of endragonèd seas.

28

But how shall I . . . make me room there:
Reach me a . . . Fancy, come faster—
Strike you the sight of it? look at it loom there,
Thing that she . . . there then! the Master,
Ipse, the only one, Christ, King, Head:
He was to cure the extremity where he had cast her;
Do, deal, lord it with living and dead;
Let him ride, her pride, in his triumph, despatch and have done
with his doom there.

29

Ah ! there was a heart right !
There was single eye !
Read the unshapeable shock night
And knew the who and the why ;
Wording it how but by him that present and past,
Heaven and earth are word of, worded by ?—
The Simon Peter of a soul ! to the blast
Tarpeian-fast, but a blown beacon of light.

30

Jesu, heart's light,
Jesu, maid's son,
What was the feast followed the night
Thou hadst glory of this nun ?—
Feast of the one woman without stain.
For so conceivèd, so to conceive thee is done ;
But here was heart-throe, birth of a brain,
Word, that heard and kept thee and uttered thee outright.

31

Well, she has thee for the pain, for the
Patience ; but pity of the rest of them !
Heart, go and bleed at a bitterer vein for the
Comfortless unconfessed of them—
No not uncomforted : lovely-felicitous Providence
Finger of a tender of, O of a feathery delicacy, the breast of the
Maiden could obey so, be a bell to, ring of it, and
Startle the poor sheep back ! is the shipwrack then a harvest,
does tempest carry the grain for thee ?

32

I admire thee, master of the tides,
Of the Yore-flood, of the year's fall;
The recurb and the recovery of the gulf's sides,
The girth of it and the wharf of it and the wall;
Stanching, quenching ocean of a motionable mind;
Ground of being, and granite of it: past all
Grasp God, throned behind
Death with a sovereignty that heeds but hides, bodes but abides;

33

With a mercy that outrides
The all of water, an ark
For the listener; for the lingerer with a love glides
Lower than death and the dark;
A vein for the visiting of the past-prayer, pent in prison,
The-last-breath penitent spirits—the uttermost mark
Our passion-plungèd giant risen,
The Christ of the Father compassionate, fetched in the storm of
his strides.

34

Now burn, new born to the world,
Doubled-naturèd name,
The heaven-flung, heart-fleshed, maiden-furled
Miracle-in-Mary-of-flame,
Mid-numbered He in three of the thunder-throne!
Not a dooms-day dazzle in his coming nor dark as he came;
Kind, but royally reclaiming his own;
A released shower, let flash to the shire, not a lightning of fire
hard-hurled.

35

Dame, at our door
Drowned, and among our shoals,
Remember us in the roads, the heaven-haven of the
Reward:
Our King back, oh, upon English souls!
Let him easter in us, be a dayspring to the dimness of us,
be a crimson-cresseted east,
More brightening her, rare-dear Britain, as his reign rolls,
Pride, rose, prince, hero of us, high-priest,
Our hearts' charity's hearth's fire, our thoughts' chivalry's throng's
Lord.

5

Penmaen Pool

For the Visitors' Book at the Inn

Who long for rest, who look for pleasure
Away from counter, court, or school
O where live well your lease of leisure
But here at, here at Penmaen Pool?

You'll dare the Alp? you'll dart the skiff?—
Each sport has here its tackle and tool:
Come, plant the staff by Cadair cliff;
Come, swing the sculls on Penmaen Pool.

What's yonder?—Grizzled Dyphwys dim:
The triple-hummocked Giant's stool,
Hoar messmate, hobs and nobs with him
To halve the bowl of Penmaen Pool.

And all the landscape under survey,
At tranquil turns, by nature's rule,
Rides repeated topsyturvy
In frank, in fairy Penmaen Pool.

And Charles's Wain, the wondrous seven,
And sheep-flock clouds like worlds of wool,
For all they shine so, high in heaven,
Shew brighter shaken in Penmaen Pool.

The Mawddach, how she trips! though throttled
If floodtide teeming thrills her full,
And mazy sands all water-wattled
Waylay her at ebb, past Penmaen Pool.

But what's to see in stormy weather,
When grey showers gather and gusts are cool?—
Why, raindrop-roundels looped together
That lace the face of Penmaen Pool.

Then even in weariest wintry hour
Of New Year's month or surly Yule
Furred snows, charged tuft above tuft, tower
From darksome darksome Penmaen Pool.

And ever, if bound here hardest home,
You've parlour-pastime left and (who'll
Not honour it?) ale like goldy foam
That frocks an oar in Penmaen Pool.

Then come who pine for peace or pleasure
Away from counter, court, or school,
Spend here your measure of time and treasure
And taste the treats of Penmaen Pool.

6

The Silver Jubilee:

To James First Bishop of Shrewsbury on the 25th Year of his Episcopate July 28, 1876

1

THOUGH no high-hung bells or din
Of braggart bugles cry it in—
   What is sound ?   Nature's round
Makes the Silver Jubilee.

2

Five and twenty years have run
Since sacred fountains to the sun
   Sprang, that but now were shut,
Showering Silver Jubilee.

3

Feasts, when we shall fall asleep,
Shrewsbury may see others keep ;
   None but you this her true,
This her Silver Jubilee.

4

Not today we need lament
Your wealth of life is some way spent :
   Toil has shed round your head
Silver but for Jubilee.

5

Then for her whose velvet vales
Should have pealed with welcome, Wales,
   Let the chime of a rhyme
Utter Silver Jubilee.

7
God's Grandeur

THE world is charged with the grandeur of God.
　　It will flame out, like shining from shook foil ;
　　It gathers to a greatness, like the ooze of oil
Crushed.　Why do men then now not reck his rod ?
Generations have trod, have trod, have trod ;
　　And all is seared with trade ; bleared, smeared with
　　　　toil ;
　　And wears man's smudge and shares man's smell :
　　　　the soil
Is bare now, nor can foot feel, being shod.

And for all this, nature is never spent ;
　　There lives the dearest freshness deep down things ;
And though the last lights off the black West went
　　Oh, morning, at the brown brink eastward, springs—
Because the Holy Ghost over the bent
　　World broods with warm breast and with ah !
　　　　bright wings.

8
The Starlight Night

LOOK at the stars ! look, look up at the skies !
　　O look at all the fire-folk sitting in the air !
　　The bright boroughs, the circle-citadels there !
Down in dim woods the diamond delves ! the elves'-eyes !
The grey lawns cold where gold, where quickgold lies !
　　Wind-beat whitebeam ! airy abeles set on a flare !
　　Flake-doves sent floating forth at a farmyard scare !—
Ah well ! it is all a purchase, all is a prize.

Buy then! bid then!—What?—Prayer, patience, alms,
    vows.
Look, look: a May-mess, like on orchard boughs!
    Look! March-bloom, like on mealed-with-yellow
      sallows!
These are indeed the barn; withindoors house
The shocks.   This piece-bright paling shuts the spouse
    Christ home, Christ and his mother and all his
      hallows.

9

Spring

NOTHING is so beautiful as spring—
    When weeds, in wheels, shoot long and lovely and lush;
    Thrush's eggs look little low heavens, and thrush
Through the echoing timber does so rinse and wring
The ear, it strikes like lightnings to hear him sing;
    The glassy peartree leaves and blooms, they brush
    The descending blue; that blue is all in a rush
With richness; the racing lambs too have fair their fling.

What is all this juice and all this joy?
    A strain of the earth's sweet being in the beginning
In Eden garden.—Have, get, before it cloy,
    Before it cloud, Christ, lord, and sour with sinning,
Innocent mind and Mayday in girl and boy,
    Most, O maid's child, thy choice and worthy the
      winning.

10

The Lantern out of Doors

SOMETIMES a lantern moves along the night,
  That interests our eyes.   And who goes there?
  I think; where from and bound, I wonder, where,
With, all down darkness wide, his wading light?

Men go by me whom either beauty bright
  In mould or mind or what not else makes rare:
  They rain against our much-thick and marsh air
Rich beams, till death or distance buys them quite.

Death or distance soon consumes them: wind
  What most I may eye after, be in at the end
I cannot, and out of sight is out of mind.

Christ minds; Christ's interest, what to avow or amend
  There, éyes them, heart wánts, care haúnts, foot
    fóllows kínd,
Their ránsom, théir rescue, ánd first, fást, last friénd.

11

The Sea and the Skylark

ON ear and ear two noises too old to end
  Trench—right, the tide that ramps against the shore;
  With a flood or a fall, low lull-off or all roar,
Frequenting there while moon shall wear and wend.

Left hand, off land, I hear the lark ascend,
  His rash-fresh re-winded new-skeinèd score
  In crisps of curl off wild winch whirl, and pour
And pelt music, till none's to spill nor spend.

How these two shame this shallow and frail town !
   How ring right out our sordid turbid time,
Being pure !   We, life's pride and cared-for crown,

   Have lost that cheer and charm of earth's past prime :
Our make and making break, are breaking, down
   To man's last dust, drain fast towards man's first slime.

12

The Windhover :

To Christ our Lord

I CAUGHT this morning morning's minion, king-
   dom of daylight's dauphin, dapple-dawn-drawn Fal-
     con, in his riding
   Of the rolling level underneath him steady air, and
     striding
High there, how he rung upon the rein of a wimpling wing
In his ecstasy ! then off, off forth on swing,
   As a skate's heel sweeps smooth on a bow-bend : the
     hurl and gliding
   Rebuffed the big wind.   My heart in hiding
Stirred for a bird,—the achieve of, the mastery of the
     thing !

Brute beauty and valour and act, oh, air, pride, plume, here
   Buckle ! AND the fire that breaks from thee then, a
     billion
Times told lovelier, more dangerous, O my chevalier !

   No wonder of it : shéer plód makes plough down
     sillion
Shine, and blue-bleak embers, ah my dear,
   Fall, gall themselves, and gash gold-vermilion.

13

Pied Beauty

GLORY be to God for dappled things—
    For skies of couple-colour as a brinded cow;
        For rose-moles all in stipple upon trout that swim;
Fresh-firecoal chestnut-falls; finches' wings;
    Landscape plotted and pieced—fold, fallow, and
        plough;
        And áll trádes, their gear and tackle and trim.

All things counter, original, spare, strange;
    Whatever is fickle, freckled (who knows how?)
        With swift, slow; sweet, sour; adazzle, dim;
He fathers-forth whose beauty is past change:
                Praise him.

14

Hurrahing in Harvest

SUMMER ends now; now, barbarous in beauty, the
        stooks arise
    Around; up above, what wind-walks! what lovely
        behaviour
Of silk-sack clouds! has wilder, wilful-wavier
Meal-drift moulded ever and melted across skies?

I walk, I lift up, I lift up heart, eyes,
    Down all that glory in the heavens to glean our
        Saviour;
    And, éyes, heárt, what looks, what lips yet gave you a
Rapturous love's greeting of realer, of rounder replies?

And the azurous hung hills are his world-wielding
    shoulder
  Majestic—as a stallion stalwart, very-violet-sweet!—
These things, these things were here and but the
    beholder
  Wanting; which two when they once meet,
The heart rears wings bold and bolder
  And hurls for him, O half hurls earth for him off
    under his feet.

15

The Caged Skylark

As a dare-gale skylark scanted in a dull cage
  Man's mounting spirit in his bone-house, mean house,
    dwells—
  That bird beyond the remembering his free fells;
This in drudgery, day-labouring-out life's age.

Though aloft on turf or perch or poor low stage,
  Both sing sometimes the sweetest, sweetest spells,
  Yet both droop deadly sómetimes in their cells
Or wring their barriers in bursts of fear or rage.

Not that the sweet-fowl, song-fowl, needs no rest—
Why, hear him, hear him babble and drop down to his nest,
  But his own nest, wild nest, no prison.

Man's spirit will be flesh-bound when found at best,
But uncumbered : meadow-down is not distressed
  For a rainbow footing it nor he for his bónes rísen.

16

In the Valley of the Elwy

I REMEMBER a house where all were good
  To me, God knows, deserving no such thing :
  Comforting smell breathed at very entering,
Fetched fresh, as I suppose, off some sweet wood.
That cordial air made those kind people a hood
    All over, as a bevy of eggs the mothering wing
    Will, or mild nights the new morsels of spring :
Why, it seemed of course ; seemed of right it should.

Lovely the woods, waters, meadows, combes, vales,
All the air things wear that build this world of Wales ;
  Only the inmate does not correspond :
God, lover of souls, swaying considerate scales,
Complete thy creature dear O where it fails,
  Being mighty a master, being a father and fond.

17

The Loss of the Eurydice

Foundered March 24, 1878

THE Eurydice—it concerned thee, O Lord :
Three hundred souls, O alas ! on board,
    Some asleep unawakened, all un-
warned, eleven fathoms fallen

4

Where she foundered!   One stroke
Felled and furled them, the hearts of oak !
   And flockbells off the aerial
Downs' forefalls beat to the burial.   8

For did she pride her, freighted fully, on
Bounden bales or a hoard of bullion?——
   Precious passing measure,
Lads and men her lade and treasure.   12

She had come from a cruise, training seamen —
Men, boldboys soon to be men :
   Must it, worst weather,
Blast bole and bloom together ?   16

No Atlantic squall overwrought her
Or rearing billow of the Biscay water :
   Home was hard at hand
And the blow bore from land.   20

And you were a liar, O blue March day.
Bright sun lanced fire in the heavenly bay ;
   But what black Boreas wrecked her ? he
Came equipped, deadly-electric,   24

A beetling baldbright cloud thorough England
Riding : there did storms not mingle ? and
   Hailropes hustle and grind their
Heavengravel ? wolfsnow, worlds of it, wind there? 28

Now Carisbrook keep goes under in gloom ;
Now it overvaults Appledurcombe ;
   Now near by Ventnor town
It hurls, hurls off Boniface Down.   32

Too proud, too proud, what a press she bore !
Royal, and all her royals wore.
    Sharp with her, shorten sail !
Too late ; lost ; gone with the gale.   36

This was that fell capsize,
As half she had righted and hoped to rise
    Death teeming in by her portholes
Raced down decks, round messes of mortals.   40

Then a lurch forward, frigate and men ;
' All hands for themselves ' the cry ran then ;
    But she who had housed them thither
Was around them, bound them or wound them with her. 44

Marcus Hare, high her captain,
Kept to her—care-drowned and wrapped in
    Cheer's death, would follow   47
His charge through the champ-white water-in-a-wallow,

All under Channel to bury in a beach her
Cheeks : Right, rude of feature,
    He thought he heard say
' Her commander ! and thou too, and thou this way.' 52

It is even seen, time 's something server,
In mankind's medley a duty-swerver,
    At downright ' No or yes ? '
Doffs all, drives full for righteousness.   56

Sydney Fletcher, Bristol-bred,
(Low lie his mates now on watery bed)
    Takes to the seas and snows
As sheer down the ship goes.   60

Now her afterdraught gullies him too down;
Now he wrings for breath with the deathgush brown;
    Till a lifebelt and God's will
Lend him a lift from the sea-swill.   64

Now he shoots short up to the round air;
Now he gasps, now he gazes everywhere;
    But his eye no cliff, no coast or
Mark makes in the rivelling snowstorm.   68

Him, after an hour of wintry waves,
A schooner sights, with another, and saves,
    And he boards her in Oh! such joy
He has lost count what came next, poor boy.—   72

They say who saw one sea-corpse cold
He was all of lovely manly mould,
    Every inch a tar,
Of the best we boast our sailors are.   76

Look, foot to forelock, how all things suit! he
Is strung by duty, is strained to beauty,
    And brown-as-dawning-skinned
With brine and shine and whirling wind.   80

O his nimble finger, his gnarled grip!
Leagues, leagues of seamanship
    Slumber in these forsaken
Bones, this sinew, and will not waken.   84

He was but one like thousands more,
Day and night I deplore
    My people and born own nation,
Fast foundering own generation.   88

I might let bygones be—our curse
Of ruinous shrine no hand or, worse,
 Robbery's hand is busy to
Dress, hoar-hallowèd shrines unvisited;   92

Only the breathing temple and fleet
Life, this wildworth blown so sweet,
 These daredeaths, ay this crew, in
Unchrist, all rolled in ruin—   96

Deeply surely I need to deplore it,
Wondering why my master bore it,
 The riving off that race
So at home, time was, to his truth and grace   100

That a starlight-wender of ours would say
The marvellous Milk was Walsingham Way
 And one—but let be, let be :
More, more than was will yet be.—   104

O well wept, mother have lost son ;
Wept, wife ; wept, sweetheart would be one :
 Though grief yield them no good
Yet shed what tears sad truelove should.   108

But to Christ lord of thunder
Crouch ; lay knee by earth low under :
 ' Holiest, loveliest, bravest,
Save my hero, O Hero savest.   112

And the prayer thou hearst me making
Have, at the awful overtaking,
 Heard ; have heard and granted
Grace that day grace was wanted.'   116

Not that hell knows redeeming,
But for souls sunk in seeming
    Fresh, till doomfire burn all,
Prayer shall fetch pity eternal.   120

18

The May Magnificat

MAY is Mary's month, and I
Muse at that and wonder why:
   ᶜ Her feasts follow reason,
    Dated due to season—

Candlemas, Lady Day;
But the Lady Month, May,
    Why fasten that upon her,
    With a feasting in her honour?

Is it only its being brighter
Than the most are must delight her?
    Is it opportunest
    And flowers finds soonest?

Ask of her, the mighty mother:
Her reply puts this other
    Question: What is Spring?—
    Growth in every thing—

Flesh and fleece, fur and feather,
Grass and greenworld all together;
    Star-eyed strawberry-breasted
    Throstle above her nested

Cluster of bugle blue eggs thin
Forms and warms the life within;
    And bird and blossom swell
    In sod or sheath or shell.

All things rising, all things sizing
Mary sees, sympathising
    With that world of good,
    Nature's motherhood.

Their magnifying of each its kind
With delight calls to mind
    How she did in her stored
    Magnify the Lord.

Well but there was more than this:
Spring's universal bliss
    Much, had much to say
    To offering Mary May.

When drop-of-blood-and-foam-dapple
Bloom lights the orchard-apple
    And thicket and thorp are merry
    With silver-surfèd cherry

And azuring-over greybell makes
Wood banks and brakes wash wet like lakes
    And magic cuckoocall
    Caps, clears, and clinches all—

This ecstasy all through mothering earth
Tells Mary her mirth till Christ's birth
    To remember and exultation
    In God who was her salvation.

19

Binsey Poplars

felled 1879

My aspens dear, whose airy cages quelled,
Quelled or quenched in **leaves** the leaping sun,
All felled, felled, are all felled;
 Of a fresh and following folded rank
   Not spared, not one
   That dandled a sandalled
  Shadow that swam or sank
On meadow and river and wind-wandering weed-winding
 bank.

O if we but knew what we do
   When we delve or hew—
 Hack and rack the growing green!
   Since country is so tender
 To touch, her being só slender,
 That, like this sleek and seeing ball
 But a prick will make no eye at all,
 Where we, even where we mean
    To mend her we end her,
   When we hew or delve:
After-comers cannot guess the beauty been.
 Ten or twelve, only ten or twelve
  Strokes of havoc únselve
   The sweet especial scene,
  Rural scene, a rural scene,
  Sweet especial rural scene.

20

Duns Scotus's Oxford

TOWERY city and branchy between towers;
Cuckoo-echoing, bell-swarmèd, lark-charmèd, rook-
    racked, river-rounded;
The dapple-eared lily below thee; that country and
    town did
Once encounter in. here coped and poisèd powers;

Thou hast a base and brickish skirt there, sours
That neighbour-nature thy grey beauty is grounded
Best in; graceless growth, thou hast confounded
Rural rural keeping—folk, flocks, and flowers.

Yet ah! this air I gather and I release
He lived on; these weeds and waters, these walls are what
He haunted who of all men most sways my spirits to
    peace;

Of realty the rarest-veinèd unraveller; a not
Rivalled insight, be rival Italy or Greece;
Who fired France for Mary without spot.

21

Henry Purcell

*The poet wishes well to the divine genius of Purcell
and praises him that, whereas other musicians have given
utterance to the moods of man's mind, he has, beyond
that, uttered in notes the very make and species of man as
created both in him and in all men generally.*

HAVE fair fallen, O fair, fair have fallen, so dear
To me, so arch-especial a spirit as heaves in Henry Purcell,
An age is now since passed, since parted ; with the reversal
Of the outward sentence low lays him, listed to a heresy,
    here.

Not mood in him nor meaning, proud fire or sacred fear,
Or love or pity or all that sweet notes not his might nursle :
It is the forgèd feature finds me ; it is the rehearsal
Of own, of abrupt self there so thrusts on, so throngs
    the ear.

Let him oh ! with his air of angels then lift me, lay me !
    only I'll
Have an eye to the sakes of him, quaint moonmarks, to
    his pelted plumage under
Wings : so some great stormfowl, whenever he has walked
    his while

The thunder-purple seabeach plumèd purple-of-thunder,
If a wuthering of his palmy snow-pinions scatter a
    colossal smile
Off him, but meaning motion fans fresh our wits with
    wonder.

22

Peace

WHEN will you ever, Peace, wild wooddove, shy wings
    shut,
Your round me roaming end, and under be my boughs?
When, when, Peace, will you, Peace? I'll not play
    hypocrite
To own my heart: I yield you do come sometimes; but
That piecemeal peace is poor peace. What pure peace
    allows
Alarms of wars, the daunting wars, the death of it?

O surely, reaving Peace, my Lord should leave in lieu
Some good! And so he does leave Patience exquisite,
That plumes to Peace thereafter. And when Peace here
    does house
He comes with work to do, he does not come to coo,
       He comes to brood and sit.

23

The Bugler's First Communion

A BUGLER boy from barrack (it is over the hill
There)—boy bugler, born, he tells me, of Irish
       Mother to an English sire (he
Shares their best gifts surely, fall how things will),

This very very day came down to us after a boon he on
My late being there begged of me, overflowing
        Boon in my bestowing,
Came, I say, this day to it—to a First Communion.

Here he knelt then ín regimental red.
Forth Christ from cupboard fetched, how fain I of feet
        To his youngster take his treat!
Low-latched in leaf-light housel his too huge godhead.

There! and your sweetest sendings, ah divine,
By it, heavens, befall him! as a heart Christ's darling,
    dauntless;
        Tongue true, vaunt- and tauntless;
Breathing bloom of a chastity in mansex fine.

Frowning and forefending angel-warder
Squander the hell-rook ranks sally to molest him;
        March, kind comrade, abreast him;
Dress his days to a dexterous and starlight order.

How it dóes my heart good, visiting at that bleak hill,
When limber liquid youth, that to all I teach
        Yields tender as a pushed peach,
Hies headstrong to its wellbeing of a self-wise self-will!

Then though I should tread tufts of consolation
Dáys áfter, só I in a sort deserve to
        And do serve God to serve to
Just such slips of soldiery Christ's royal ration.

Nothing élse is like it, no, not all so strains
Us: fresh youth fretted in a bloomfall all portending
        That sweet's sweeter ending;
Realm both Christ is heir to and thére réigns.

O now well work that sealing sacred ointment!
O for now charms, arms, what bans off bad
        And locks love ever in a lad!
Let mé though see no more of him, and not disappointment

Those sweet hopes quell whose least me quickenings lift,
In scarlet or somewhere of some day seeing
        That brow and bead of being,
An our day's God's own Galahad.   Though this child's
    drift

Seems by a divíne doom chánnelled, nor do I cry
Disaster there; but may he not rankle and roam
        In backwheels though bound home?—
That left to the Lord of the Eucharist, I here lie by;

Recorded only, I have put my lips on pleas
Would brandle adamantine heaven with ride and jar, did
        Prayer go disregarded:
Forward-like, but however, and like favourable heaven
    heard these.

24

Morning Midday and Evening Sacrifice

THE dappled die-away
Cheek and wimpled lip,
The gold-wisp, the airy-grey
Eye, all in fellowship—
This, all this beauty blooming,
This, all this freshness fuming,
Give God while worth consuming.

Both thought and thew now bolder
And told by Nature : Tower ;
Head, heart, hand, heel, and shoulder
That beat and breathe in power—
This pride of prime's enjoyment
Take as for tool, not toy meant
And hold at Christ's employment.

The vault and scope and schooling
And mastery in the mind,
In silk-ash kept from cooling,
And ripest under rind—
What life half lifts the latch of,
What hell stalks towards the snatch of,
Your offering, with despatch, of !

25

Andromeda

Now Time's Andromeda on this rock rude,
With not her either beauty's equal or
Her injury's, looks off by both horns of shore,
Her flower, her piece of being, doomed dragon's food.

    Time past she has been attempted and pursued
By many blows and banes ; but now hears roar
A wilder beast from West than all were, more
Rife in her wrongs, more lawless, and more lewd.

    Her Perseus linger and leave her tó her extremes ?—
Pillowy air he treads a time and hangs
His thoughts on her, forsaken that she seems,
    All while her patience, morselled into pangs,
Mounts ; then to alight disarming, no one dreams,
With Gorgon's gear and barebill, thongs and fangs.

26

The Candle Indoors

Some candle clear burns somewhere I come by.
I muse at how its being puts blissful back
With yellowy moisture mild night's blear-all black,
Or to-fro tender trambeams truckle at the eye.
By that window what task what fingers ply,
I plod wondering, a-wanting, just for lack
Of answer the eagerer a-wanting Jessy or Jack
There   God to aggrándise, God to glorify.—

Come you indoors, come home ; your fading fire
Mend first and vital candle in close heart's vault :
You there are master, do your own desire ;
What hinders ? Are you beam-blind, yet to a fault
In a neighbour deft-handed ? are you that liar
And, cast by conscience out, spendsavour salt ?

27

The Handsome Heart:

at a Gracious Answer

'But tell me, child, your choice ; what shall I buy
You ?'—'Father, what you buy me I like best.'
With the sweetest air that said, still plied and pressed,
He swung to his first poised purport of reply.

What the heart is ! which, like carriers let fly—
Doff darkness, homing nature knows the rest—
To its own fine function, wild and self-instressed,
Falls light as ten years long taught how to and why.

Mannerly-hearted ! more than handsome face—
Beauty's bearing or muse of mounting vein,
All, in this case, bathed in high hallowing grace . . .

Of heaven what boon to buy you, boy, or gain
Not granted !—Only . . . O on that path you pace
Run all your race, O brace sterner that strain !

28

At the Wedding March

God with honour hang your head,
Groom, and grace you, bride, your bed
With lissome scions, sweet scions,
Out of hallowed bodies bred.

Each be other's comfort kind :
Déep, déeper than divined,
Divine charity, dear charity,
Fast you ever, fast bind.

Then let the march tread our ears :
I to him turn with tears
Who to wedlock, his wonder wedlock,
Déals tríumph and immortal years.

29

Felix Randal

FELIX RANDAL the farrier, O he is dead then ? my duty all ended,
Who have watched his mould of man, big-boned and hardy-
    handsome
Pining, pining, till time when reason rambled in it and some
Fatal four disorders, fleshed there, all contended ?

Sickness broke him. Impatient he cursed at first, but mended
Being anointed and all ; though a heavenlier heart began some
Months earlier, since I had our sweet reprieve and ransom
Tendered to him. Ah well, God rest him all road ever he
    offended !

This seeing the sick endears them to us, us too it endears.
My tongue had taught thee comfort, touch had quenched thy tears,
Thy tears that touched my heart, child, Felix, poor Felix Randal;

How far from then forethought of, all thy more boisterous years,
When thou at the random grim forge, powerful amidst peers,
Didst fettle for the great grey drayhorse his bright and battering
    sandal !

30
Brothers

How lovely the elder brother's
Life all laced in the other's,
Lóve-laced!——what once I well
Witnessed; so fortune fell.
When Shrovetide, two years gone,   5
Our boys' plays brought on
Part was picked for John,
Young Jóhn: then fear, then joy
Ran revel in the elder boy.
Their night was come now; all   10
Our company thronged the hall;
Henry, by the wall,
Beckoned me beside him:
I came where called, and eyed him
By meanwhiles; making mý play   15
Turn most on tender byplay.
For, wrung all on love's rack,
My lad, and lost in Jack,
Smiled, blushed, and bit his lip;
Or drove, with a diver's dip,   20
Clutched hands down through clasped knees——
Truth's tokens tricks like these,
Old telltales, with what stress
He hung on the imp's success.
Now the other was bráss-bóld: 25
Hé had no work to hold
His heart up at the strain;
Nay, roguish ran the vein.
Two tedious acts were past;
Jack's call and cue at last;   30
When Henry, heart-forsook,
Dropped eyes and dared not look.

Eh, how áll rúng!
Young dog, he did give tongue!
But Harry—in his hands he has flung   35
His tear-tricked cheeks of flame
For fond love and for shame.
    Ah Nature, framed in fault,
There's comfort then, there's salt;
Nature, bad, base, and blind,   40
Dearly thou canst be kind;
There dearly thén, deárly,
I'll cry thou canst be kind.

31

Spring and Fall:

to a young child

MÁRGARÉT, are you gríeving
Over Goldengrove unleaving?
Leáves, líke the things of man, you
With your fresh thoughts care for, can you?
Áh! ás the heart grows older
It will come to such sights colder
By and by, nor spare a sigh
Though worlds of wanwood leafmeal lie;
And yet you wíll weep and know why.
Now no matter, child, the name:
Sórrow's spríngs áre the same.
Nor mouth had, no nor mind, expressed
What heart heard of, ghost guessed:
It ís the blight man was born for,
It is Margaret you mourn for.

32

Spelt from Sibyl's Leaves

Earnest, earthless, equal, attuneable, ˈ vaulty, voluminous, . .
  stupendous
Evening strains to be tíme's vást, ˈ womb-of-all, home-of-all,
  hearse-of-all night.
Her fond yellow hornlight wound to the west, ˈ her wild hollow
  hoarlight hung to the height
Waste ; her earliest stars, earl-stars, ˈ stárs principal, overbend us,
Fíre-féaturing heaven. For earth ˈ her being has unbound, her
  dapple is at an end, as-
tray or aswarm, all throughther, in throngs ; ˈ self ín self steepèd
  and páshed—qúite
Disremembering, dísmémbering ˈ áll now. Heart, you round me
  right
With : Óur évening is over us ; óur night ˈ whélms, whélms, ánd
  will end us.
Only the beak-leaved boughs dragonish ˈ damask the tool-smooth
  bleak light ; black,
Ever so black on it. Óur tale, O óur oracle ! ˈ Lét life, wáned,
  ah lét life wind
Off hér once skéined stained véined varíety ˈ upon, áll on twó
  spools ; párt, pen, páck
Now her áll in twó flocks, twó folds—black, white ; ˈ right,
  wrong ; reckon but, reck but, mind
But thése two ; wáre of a wórld where bút these ˈ twó tell, each
  off the óther ; of a rack
Where, selfwrung, selfstrung, sheathe- and shelterless, ˈ thóughts
  agaínst thoughts ín groans grínd.

33

Inversnaid

THIS darksome burn, horseback brown,
His rollrock highroad roaring down,
In coop and in comb the fleece of his foam
Flutes and low to the lake falls home.

A windpuff-bonnet of fáwn-fróth
Turns and twindles over the broth
Of a pool so pitchblack, féll-frówning,
It rounds and rounds Despair to drowning.

Degged with dew, dappled with dew
Are the groins of the braes that the brook treads through,
Wiry heathpacks, flitches of fern,
And the beadbonny ash that sits over the burn.

What would the world be, once bereft
Of wet and of wildness? Let them be left,
O let them be left, wildness and wet;
Long live the weeds and the wilderness yet.

34

As kingfishers catch fire, dragonflies dráw fláme ;
As tumbled over rim in roundy wells
Stones ring; like each tucked string tells, each hung bell's
Bow swung finds tongue to fling out broad its name ;
Each mortal thing does one thing and the same :
Deals out that being indoors each one dwells ;
Selves—goes itself; *myself* it speaks and spells,
Crying *Whát I do is me : for that I came.*

Í say móre : the just man justices ;
Kéeps gráce : thát keeps all his goings graces ;
Acts in God's eye what in God's eye he is—
Chríst—for Christ plays in ten thousand places,
Lovely in limbs, and lovely in eyes not his
To the Father through the features of men's faces.

35

Ribblesdale

EARTH, sweet Earth, sweet landscape, with leavès throng
And louchèd low grass, heaven that dost appeal
To, with no tongue to plead, no heart to feel ;
That canst but only be, but dost that long—

Thou canst but be, but that thou well dost ; strong
Thy plea with him who dealt, nay does now deal,
Thy lovely dale down thus and thus bids reel
Thy river, and o'er gives all to rack or wrong.

And what is Earth's eye, tongue, or heart else, where
Else, but in dear and dogged man?—Ah, the heir
To his own selfbent so bound, so tied to his turn,
To thriftless reave both our rich round world bare
And none reck of world after, this bids wear
Earth brows of such care, care and dear concern.

36

The Leaden Echo and the Golden Echo

(*Maidens' song from St. Winefred's Well*)

THE LEADEN ECHO

How to keep—is there ány any, is there none such, nowhere
    known some, bow or brooch or braid or brace, láce, latch
    or catch or key to keep
Back beauty, keep it, beauty, beauty, beauty, . . . from vanishing
    away?
Ó is there no frowning of these wrinkles, rankèd wrinkles deep,
Dówn? no waving off of these most mournful messengers, still
    messengers, sad and stealing messengers of grey?
No there's none, there's none, O no there's none,
Nor can you long be, what you now are, called fair,
Do what you may do, what, do what you may,
And wisdom is early to despair:
Be beginning; since, no, nothing can be done
To keep at bay
Age and age's evils, hoar hair,
Ruck and wrinkle, drooping, dying, death's worst, winding
    sheets, tombs and worms and tumbling to decay;

So be beginning, be beginning to despair.
O there's none ; no no no there's none :
Be beginning to despair, to despair,
Despair, despair, despair, despair.

The Golden Echo

      Spare !
There is one, yes I have one (Hush there !) ;
Only not within seeing of the sun,
Not within the singeing of the strong sun,
Tall sun's tingeing, or treacherous the tainting of the earth's air,
Somewhere elsewhere there is ah well where ! one,
One. Yes I can tell such a key, I do know such a place,
Where whatever's prized and passes of us, everything that's
      fresh and fast flying of us, seems to us sweet of us and
      swiftly away with, done away with, undone,
Undone, done with, soon done with, and yet dearly and
      dangerously sweet
Of us, the wimpled-water-dimpled, not-by-morning-matchèd face,
The flower of beauty, fleece of beauty, too too apt to, ah! to fleet,
Never fleets móre, fastened with the tenderest truth
To its own best being and its loveliness of youth : it is an ever-
      lastingness of, O it is an all youth !
Come then, your ways and airs and looks, locks, maiden gear,
      gallantry and gaiety and grace,
Winning ways, airs innocent, maiden manners, sweet looks,
      loose locks, long locks, lovelocks, gaygear, going gallant,
      girlgrace—
Resign them, sign them, seal them, send them, motion them
      with breath,
And with sighs soaring, soaring síghs deliver
Them ; beauty-in-the-ghost, deliver it, early now, long before
      death
Give beauty back, beauty, beauty, beauty, back to God, beauty's
      self and beauty's giver.

See; not a hair is, not an eyelash, not the least lash lost; every hair
Is, hair of the head, numbered.
Nay, what we had lighthanded left in surly the mere mould
Will have waked and have waxed and have walked with the wind
      what while we slept,
This side, that side hurling a heavyheaded hundredfold
What while we, while we slumbered.
O then, weary then whý should we tread? O why are we so
      haggard at the heart, so care-coiled, care-killed, so fagged,
      so fashed, so cogged, so cumbered,
When the thing we freely fórfeit is kept with fonder a care,
Fonder a care kept than we could have kept it, kept
Far with fonder a care (and we, we should have lost it) finer, fonder
A care kept.—Where kept? Do but tell us where kept, where.—
Yonder.—What high as that! We follow, now we follow.—
    Yonder, yes yonder, yonder,
Yonder.

37

The Blessed Virgin compared to the Air we Breathe

WILD air, world-mothering air,
Nestling me everywhere,
That each eyelash or hair
Girdles; goes home betwixt
The fleeciest, frailest-flixed
Snowflake; that's fairly mixed
With, riddles, and is rife
In every least thing's life;
This needful, never spent,
And nursing element;   10

My more than meat and drink,
My meal at every wink;
This air, which, by life's law,
My lung must draw and draw
Now but to breathe its praise,
Minds me in many ways
Of her who not only
Gave God's infinity
Dwindled to infancy
Welcome in womb and breast,   20
Birth, milk, and all the rest
But mothers each new grace
That does now reach our race—
Mary Immaculate,
Merely a woman, yet
Whose presence, power is
Great as no goddess's
Was deemèd, dreamèd; who
This one work has to do—
Let all God's glory through,   30
God's glory which would go
Through her and from her flow
Off, and no way but so.

      I say that we are wound
With mercy round and round
As if with air: the same
Is Mary, more by name.
She, wild web, wondrous robe,
Mantles the guilty globe,
Since God has let dispense   40
Her prayers his providence:
Nay, more than almoner,
The sweet alms' self is her
And men are meant to share

Her life as life does air.
    If I have understood,
She holds high motherhood
Towards all our ghostly good
And plays in grace her part
About man's beating heart,   50
Laying, like air's fine flood,
The deathdance in his blood;
Yet no part but what will
Be Christ our Saviour still.
Of her flesh he took flesh:
He does take fresh and fresh,
Though much the mystery how,
Not flesh but spirit now
And makes, O marvellous!
New Nazareths in us,   60
Where she shall yet conceive
Him, morning, noon, and eve;
New Bethlems, and he born
There, evening, noon, and morn—
Bethlem or Nazareth,
Men here may draw like breath
More Christ and baffle death;
Who, born so, comes to be
New self and nobler me
In each one and each one   70
More makes, when all is done,
Both God's and Mary's Son.
      Again, look overhead
How air is azurèd;
O how! nay do but stand
Where you can lift your hand
Skywards: rich, rich it laps
Round the four fingergaps.
Yet such a sapphire-shot,

Charged, steepèd sky will not   80
Stain light.   Yea, mark you this:
It does no prejudice.
The glass-blue days are those
When every colour glows,
Each shape and shadow shows.
Blue be it: this blue heaven
The seven or seven times seven
Hued sunbeam will transmit
Perfect, not alter it.
Or if there does some soft,   90
On things aloof, aloft,
Bloom breathe, that one breath more
Earth is the fairer for.
Whereas did air not make
This bath of blue and slake
His fire, the sun would shake,
A blear and blinding ball
With blackness bound, and all
The thick stars round him roll
Flashing like flecks of coal,   100
Quartz-fret, or sparks of salt,
In grimy vasty vault.
        So God was god of old:
A mother came to mould
Those limbs like ours which are
What must make our daystar
Much dearer to mankind;
Whose glory bare would blind
Or less would win man's mind.
Through her we may see him   110
Made sweeter, not made dim,
And her hand leaves his light
Sifted to suit our sight.

Be thou then, O thou dear
Mother, my atmosphere ;
My happier world, wherein
To wend and meet no sin ;
Above me, round me lie
Fronting my froward eye
With sweet and scarless sky ;
Stir in my ears, speak there
Of God's love, O live air,
Of patience, penance, prayer :
World-mothering air, air wild,
Wound with thee, in thee isled,
Fold home, fast fold thy child.

120

38

To what serves Mortal Beauty ?

To what serves mortal beauty ǀ —dangerous ; does set danc-
ing blood—the O-seal-that-so ǀ feature, flung prouder form
Than Purcell tune lets tread to ? ǀ See : it does this : keeps warm
Men's wits to the things that are ; ǀ what good means—where a glance
Master more may than gaze, ǀ gaze out of countenance.
Those lovely lads once, wet-fresh ǀ windfalls of war's storm,
How then should Gregory, a father, ǀ have gleanèd else from swarm-
ed Rome ? But God to a nation ǀ dealt that day's dear chance.
   To man, that needs would worship ǀ block or barren stone,
Our law says : Love what are ǀ love's worthiest, were all known ;
World's loveliest—men's selves. Self ǀ flashes off frame and face.
What do then ? how meet beauty ? ǀ Merely meet it ; own,
Home at heart, heaven's sweet gift ; ǀ then leave, let that alone.
Yea, wish that though, wish all, ǀ God's better beauty, grace.

39
(*The Soldier*)

YES. Whý do we áll, seeing of a soldier, bless him? bless
Our redcoats, our tars? Both these being, the greater part,
But frail clay, nay but foul clay. Here it is: the heart,
Since, proud, it calls the calling manly, gives a guess
That, hopes that, makesbelieve, the men must be no less;
It fancies, feigns, deems, dears the artist after his art;
And fain will find as sterling all as all is smart,
And scarlet wear the spirit of wár thére express.

Mark Christ our King. He knows war, served this soldiering
      through;
He of all can handle a rope best. There he bides in bliss
Now, and séeing somewhére some mán do all that man can do,
For love he leans forth, needs his neck must fall on, kiss,
And cry 'O Christ-done deed! So God-made-flesh does too:
Were I come o'er again' cries Christ 'it should be this'.

40
(*Carrion Comfort*)

NOT, I'll not, carrion comfort, Despair, not feast on thee;
Not untwist— slack they may be—these last strands of man
In me ór, most weary, cry *I can no more*. I can;
Can something, hope, wish day come, not choose not to be.
But ah, but O thou terrible, why wouldst thou rude on me
Thy wring-world right foot rock? lay a lionlimb against
      me? scan
With darksome devouring eyes my bruisèd bones? and fan,
O in turns of tempest, me heaped there; me frantic to
      avoid thee and flee?

Why?   That my chaff might fly; my grain lie, sheer
    and clear.
Nay in all that toil, that coil, since (seems) I kissed the rod,
Hand rather, my heart lo! lapped strength, stole joy,
    would laugh, chéer.
Cheer whom though? the hero whose heaven-handling
    flung me, fóot tród
Me? or me that fought him? O which one? is it each
    one? That night, that year
Of now done darkness I wretch lay wrestling with (my
    God!) my God.

41

No worst, there is none.   Pitched past pitch of grief,
More pangs will, schooled at forepangs, wilder wring.
Comforter, where, where is your comforting?
Mary, mother of us, where is your relief?
My cries heave, herds-long; huddle in a main, a chief
Woe, world-sorrow; on an age-old anvil wince and sing—
Then lull, then leave off. Fury had shrieked 'No ling-
ering!   Let me be fell: force I must be brief'.

  O the mind, mind has mountains; cliffs of fall
Frightful, sheer, no-man-fathomed. Hold them cheap
May who ne'er hung there.   Nor does long our small
Durance deal with that steep or deep.   Here! creep,
Wretch, under a comfort serves in a whirlwind: all
Life death does end and each day dies with sleep.

42

Tom's Garland:

upon the Unemployed

TOM—garlanded with squat and surly steel
Tom; then Tom's fallowbootfellow piles pick
By him and rips out rockfire homeforth—sturdy Dick;
Tom Heart-at-ease, Tom Navvy: he is all for his meal
Sure, 's bed now. Low be it: lustily he his low lot (feel
That ne'er need hunger, Tom; Tom seldom sick,
Seldomer heartsore; that treads through, prickproof,
     thick
Thousands of thorns, thoughts) swings though. Common-
     weal
Little I reck ho! lacklevel in, if all had bread:
What! Country is honour enough in all us—lordly head,
With heaven's lights high hung round, or, mother-ground
That mammocks, mighty foot. But no way sped,
Nor mind nor mainstrength; gold go garlanded
With, perilous, O nó; nor yet plod safe shod sound;
                    Undenizened, beyond bound
Of earth's glory, earth's ease, all; no one, nowhere,
In wide the world's weal; rare gold, bold steel, bare
                    In both; care, but share care—
This, by Despair, bred Hangdog dull; by Rage,
Manwolf, worse; and their packs infest the age.

43

Harry Ploughman

Hard as hurdle arms, with a broth of goldish flue
Breathed round; the rack of ribs; the scooped flank; lank
Rope-over thigh; knee-nave; and barrelled shank—
      Head and foot, shoulder and shank—
By a grey eye's heed steered well, one crew, fall to;
Stand at stress. Each limb's barrowy brawn, his thew
That onewhere curded, onewhere sucked or sank—
      Soared or sank—,
Though as a beechbole firm, finds his, as at a roll-
    call, rank
And features, in flesh, what deed he each must do—
      His sinew-service where do.

He leans to it, Harry bends, look. Back, elbow, and
    liquid waist
In him, all quail to the wallowing o' the plough:
    's cheek crimsons; curls
Wag or crossbridle, in a wind lifted, windlaced—
      See his wind- lilylocks -laced;
Churlsgrace, too, child of Amansstrength, how it hangs
    or hurls
Them—broad in bluff hide his frowning feet lashed! raced
With, along them, cragiron under and cold furls—
      With-a-fountain's shining-shot furls.

44

To seem the stranger lies my lot, my life
Among strangers.   Father and mother dear,
Brothers and sisters are in Christ not near
And he my peace my parting, sword and strife.

England, whose honour O all my heart woos, wife
To my creating thought, would neither hear
Me, were I pleading, plead nor do I : I wear-
y of idle a being but by where wars are rife.

I am in Ireland now; now I am at a thírd
Remove.   Not but in all removes I can
Kind love both give and get.   Only what word
Wisest my heart breeds dark heaven's baffling ban
Bars or hell's spell thwarts.   This to hoard unheard,
Heard unheeded, leaves me a lonely began.

45

I WAKE and feel the fell of dark, not day.
What hours, O what black hoürs we have spent
This night! what sights you, heart, saw; ways you went!
And more must, in yet longer light's delay.

With witness I speak this.   But where I say
Hours I mean years, mean life.   And my lament
Is cries countless, cries like dead letters sent
To dearest him that lives alas ! away.

I am gall, I am heartburn.   God's most deep decree
Bitter would have me taste : my taste was me ;
Bones built in me, flesh filled, blood brimmed the curse.
Selfyeast of spirit a dull dough sours.   I see
The lost are like this, and their scourge to be
As I am mine, their sweating selves ; but worse.

46

PATIENCE, hard thing! the hard thing but to pray,
But bid for, Patience is! Patience who asks
Wants war, wants wounds; weary his times, his tasks;
To do without, take tosses, and obey.

Rare patience roots in these, and, these away,
Nowhere.   Natural heart's ivy, Patience masks
Our ruins of wrecked past purpose.   There she basks
Purple eyes and seas of liquid leaves all day.

We hear our hearts grate on themselves: it kills
To bruise them dearer.   Yet the rebellious wills
Of us we do bid God bend to him even so.
And where is he who more and more distils
Delicious kindness?—He is patient.   Patience fills
His crisp combs, and that comes those ways we know.

47

MY own heart let me more have pity on; let
Me live to my sad self hereafter kind,
Charitable; not live this tormented mind
With this tormented mind tormenting yet.

I cast for comfort I can no more get
By groping round my comfortless, than blind
Eyes in their dark can day or thirst can find
Thirst's all-in-all in all a world of wet.

Soul, self; come, poor Jackself, I do advise
You, jaded, let be; call off thoughts awhile
Elsewhere; leave comfort root-room; let joy size
At God knows when to God knows what; whose smile
's not wrung, see you; unforeseen times rather—as skies
Betweenpie mountains—lights a lovely mile.

48

That Nature is a Heraclitean Fire and of the comfort of the Resurrection

CLOUD-PUFFBALL, torn tufts, tossed pillows ' flaunt forth, then chevy on an air-
built thoroughfare : heaven-roysterers, in gay-gangs ' they throng ; they glitter in marches.
Down roughcast, down dazzling whitewash, ' wherever an elm arches,
Shivelights and shadowtackle in long ' lashes lace, lance, and pair.
Delightfully the bright wind boisterous ' ropes, wrestles, beats earth bare
Of yestertempest's creases ; in pool and rut peel parches
Squandering ooze to squeezed ' dough, crust, dust ; stanches, starches
Squadroned masks and manmarks ' treadmire toil there
Footfretted in it.   Million-fuelèd, ' nature's bonfire burns on.
But quench her bonniest, dearest ' to her, her clearest-selvèd spark
Man, how fast his firedint, ' his mark on mind, is gone !
Both are in an unfathomable, all is in an enormous dark
Drowned.   O pity and indig ' nation !   Manshape, that shone
Sheer off, disseveral, a star, ' death blots black out ; nor mark
         Is any of him at all so stark
But vastness blurs and time ' beats level.   Enough ! the Resurrection,
A heart's-clarion !   Away grief's gasping, ' joyless days, dejection.
         Across my foundering deck shone
A beacon, an eternal beam. ' Flesh fade, and mortal trash
Fall to the residuary worm ; ' world's wildfire, leave but ash :
         In a flash, at a trumpet crash,
I am all at once what Christ is, ' since he was what I am, and
This Jack, joke, poor potsherd, ' patch, matchwood, immortal diamond,
         Is immortal diamond.

49

In honour of

St. Alphonsus Rodriguez

Laybrother of the Society of Jesus

HONOUR is flashed off exploit, so we say;
And those strokes once that gashed flesh or galled shield
Should tongue that time now, trumpet now that field,
And, on the fighter, forge his glorious day.
On Christ they do and on the martyr may;
But be the war within, the brand we wield
Unseen, the heroic breast not outward-steeled,
Earth hears no hurtle then from fiercest fray.

Yet God (that hews mountain and continent,
Earth, all, out; who, with trickling increment,
Veins violets and tall trees makes more and more)
Could crowd career with conquest while there went
Those years and years by of world without event
That in Majorca Alfonso watched the door.

50

*Justus quidem tu es, Domine, si disputem tecum : verum-
tamen justa loquar ad te : Quare via impiorum prospera-
tur ? &c.*

THOU art indeed just, Lord, if I contend
With thee ; but, sir, so what I plead is just.
Why do sinners' ways prosper ? and why must
Disappointment all I endeavour end ?

Wert thou my enemy, O thou my friend,
How wouldst thou worse, I wonder, than thou dost
Defeat, thwart me ? Oh, the sots and thralls of lust
Do in spare hours more thrive than I that spend,
Sir, life upon thy cause. See, banks and brakes
Now, leavèd how thick ! lacèd they are again
With fretty chervil, look, and fresh wind shakes
Them ; birds build—but not I build ; no, but strain,
Time's eunuch, and not breed one work that wakes.
Mine, O thou lord of life, send my roots rain.

51

To R. B.

THE fine delight that fathers thought ; the strong
Spur, live and lancing like the blowpipe flame,
Breathes once and, quenchèd faster than it came,
Leaves yet the mind a mother of immortal song.
Nine months she then, nay years, nine years she long
Within her wears, bears, cares and moulds the same :
The widow of an insight lost she lives, with aim
Now known and hand at work now never wrong.
Sweet fire the sire of muse, my soul needs this ;
I want the one rapture of an inspiration.
O then if in my lagging lines you miss
The roll, the rise, the carol, the creation,
My winter world, that scarcely breathes that bliss
Now, yields you, with some sighs, our explanation.

UNFINISHED POEMS & FRAGMENTS

52

Summa

THE best ideal is the true
    And other truth is none.
All glory be ascribèd to
    The holy Three in One.

53

WHAT being in rank-old nature should earlier have that
    breath been
That hére pérsonal tells off these heart-song powerful
    peals ?—
A bush-browed, beetle-brówed bíllow is it?
With a soúth-wésterly wínd blústering, with a tide rolls
    reels
Of crumbling, fore-foundering, thundering all-surfy seas
    in ; seen
Únderneath, their glassy barrel, of a fairy green.
    .   .   .   .

Or a jaunting vaunting vaulting assaulting trumpet telling.

54
On the Portrait of Two Beautiful Young People

A Brother and Sister

O I admire and sorrow! The heart's eye grieves
Discovering you, dark tramplers, tyrant years.
A juice rides rich through bluebells, in vine leaves,
And beauty's dearest veriest vein is tears.

Happy the father, mother of these! Too fast:
Not that, but thus far, all with frailty, blest
In one fair fall; but, for time's aftercast,
Creatures all heft, hope, hazard, interest.

And are they thus? The fine, the fingering beams
Their young delightful hour do feature down
That fleeted else like day-dissolvèd dreams
Or ringlet-race on burling Barrow brown.

She leans on him with such contentment fond
As well the sister sits, would well the wife;
His looks, the soul's own letters, see beyond,
Gaze on, and fall directly forth on life.

But ah, bright forelock, cluster that you are
Of favoured make and mind and health and youth,
Where lies your landmark, seamark, or soul's star?
There's none but truth can stead you. Christ is truth.

There 's none but good can bé good, both for you
And what sways with you, maybe this sweet maid ;
None good but God—a warning wavèd to
One once that was found wanting when **Good** weighed.

Man lives that list, that leaning in the will
No wisdom can forecast by gauge or guess,
The selfless self of self, most strange, most still,
Fast furled and all foredrawn to No or Yes.

Your feast of ; that most in you earnest eye
May but call on your banes to more carouse.
Worst will the best.   What worm was here, we cry,
To have havoc-pocked so, see, the hung-heavenward
       boughs ?

Enough : corruption was the world's first woe.
What need I strain my heart beyond my ken ?
O but I bear my burning witness though
Against the wild and wanton work of men.

.   .   .   .   .   .

55

THE sea took pity : it interposed with doom :
' I have tall daughters dear that heed my hand :
Let Winter wed one, sow them in her womb,
And she shall child them on the New-world strand.'

.   .   .   .   .   .

56

(Ash-boughs)

a.

NOT of all my eyes see, wandering on the world,
Is anything a milk to the mind so, so sighs deep
Poetry to it, as a tree whose boughs break in the sky.
Say it is ash-boughs: whether on a December day and
    furled
Fast ór they in clammyish lashtender combs creep
Apart wide and new-nestle at heaven most high.
They touch heaven, tabour on it; how their talons sweep
The smouldering enormous winter welkin!   May
Mells blue and snow white through them, a fringe and fray
Of greenery: it is old earth's groping towards the steep
    Heaven whom she childs us by.

(*Variant from line 7.*)   *b.*

They touch, they tabour on it, hover on it[; here, there
    hurled],
    With talons sweep
The smouldering enormous winter welkin.   [Eye,
    But more cheer is when] May
Mells blue with snowwhite through their fringe and fray
Of greenery and old earth gropes for, grasps at steep
    Heaven with it whom she childs things by.

57

.   .   .   .

HOPE holds to Christ the mind's own mirror out
To take His lovely likeness more and more.
It will not well, so she would bring about
An ever brighter burnish than before

And turns to wash it from her welling eyes
And breathes the blots off all with sighs on sighs.
Her glass is blest but she as good as blind
Holds till hand aches and wonders what is there;
Her glass drinks light, she darkles down behind,
All of her glorious gainings unaware.

.　　.　　.　　.　　.　　.　　.

I told you that she turned her mirror dim
Betweenwhiles, but she sees herself not Him.

.　　.　　.　　.

58

St. Winefred's Well

ACT I.　SC. 1

Enter Teryth from riding, Winefred following.

T.　WHAT is it, Gwen, my girl? why do you hover and haunt me?
W.　You came by Caerwys, sir?
T.　　　　　　　I came by Caerwys.
W.　　　　　　　　　　There
Some messenger there might have met you from my uncle.
T.　Your uncle met the messenger—met me; and this the
　　message:
Lord Beuno comes to-night.
W.　　　　　To-night, sir!
T.　　　　　　　　Soon, now: therefore
Have all things ready in his room.
W.　　　　　　　There needs but little doing.
T.　Let what there needs be done. Stay! with him one com-
　　panion,
His deacon, Dirvan: Warm twice over must the welcome be,

But both will share one cell.—This was good news,
    Gwenvrewi.

W. Ah yes!

T.   Why, get thee gone then; tell thy mother J want her.
                                Exit Winefred.

No man has such a daughter. The fathers of the world
Call no such maiden 'mine'. The deeper grows her
    dearness
And more and more times laces round and round my heart,
The more some monstrous hand gropes with clammy fingers
    there,
Tampering with those sweet bines, draws them out, strains
    them, strains them;
Meantime some tongue cries 'What, Teryth! what, thou
    poor fond father!
How when this bloom, this honeysuckle, that rides the air
    so rich about thee,
Is all, all sheared away, thus!' Then I sweat for fear.
Or else a funeral, and yet 'tis not a funeral,
Some pageant which takes tears and I must foot with
    feeling that
Alive or dead my girl is carried in it, endlessly
Goes marching thro' my mind. What sense is this? It
    has none.
This is too much the father; nay the mother. Fanciful!
I here forbid my thoughts to fool themselves with fears.
                 Enter Gwenlo.

.   .   .   .

Act II.—*Scene, a wood ending in a steep bank over a dry dene.*
Winefred having been murdered within, re-enter Caradoc
with a bloody sword.

C. My heart, where have we been? What have we seen, my
    mind?

What stroke has Caradoc's right arm dealt? what done?
    Head of a rebel
Struck off it has; written upon lovely limbs,
In bloody letters, lessons of earnest, of revenge;
Monuments of my earnest, records of my revenge,
On one that went against me whéreas I had warned her—
Warned her! well she knew.   I warned her of this work.
What work? what harm's done?   There is no harm done,
    none yet;
Perhaps we struck no blow, Gwenvrewi lives perhaps;
To makebelieve my mood was—mock. O I might think so
But here, here is a workman from his day's task sweats.
Wiped I am sure this was; it seems not well; for still,
Still the scarlet swings and dances on the blade.
So be it.   Thou steel, thou butcher,
I cán scour thee, fresh burnish thee, sheathe thee in thy
    dark lair; these drops
Never, never, never in their blue banks again.
The woeful, Cradock, O the woeful word!   Then what,
What have we seen? Her head, sheared from her shoulders,
    fall,
And lapped in shining hair, roll to the bank's edge; then
Down the beetling banks, like water in waterfalls,
It stooped and flashed and fell and ran like water away.
Her eyes, oh and her eyes!
In all her beauty, and sunlight to it is a pit, den, dark-
    ness,
Foam-falling is not fresh to it, rainbow by it not beaming,
In all her body, I say, no place was like her eyes,
No piece matched those eyes kept most part much cast down
But, being lifted, immortal, of immortal brightness.
Several times I saw them, thrice or four times turning;
Round and round they came and flashed towards heaven:
    O there,
There they did appeal.   Therefore airy vengeances

Are afoot; heaven-vault fast purpling portends, and what
    first lightning
Any instant falls means me.   And I do not repent;
I do not and I will not repent, not repent.
The blame bear who aroused me.   What I have done violent
I have like a lion done, lionlike done,
Honouring an uncontrolled royal wrathful nature,
Mantling passion in a grandeur, crimson grandeur.
Now be my pride then perfect, all one piece.   Henceforth
In a wide world of defiance Caradoc lives alone,
Loyal to his own soul, laying his own law down, no law nor
Lord now curb him for ever. O daring! O deep insight!
What is virtue?   Valour; only the heart valiant.
And right?   Only resolution; will, his will unwavering
Who, like me, knowing his nature to the heart home,
    nature's business,
Despatches with no flinching.   But will flesh, O can flesh
Second this fiery strain?   Not always; O no no!
We cannot live this life out; sometimes we must weary
And in this darksome world what comfort can I find?
Down this darksome world cómfort whére can I find
When 'ts light I quenched; its rose, time's one rich rose,
    my hand,
By her bloom, fast by her fresh, her fleecèd bloom,
Hideous dashed down, leaving earth a winter withering
With no now, no Gwenvrewi.   I must miss her most
That might have spared her were it but for passion-sake. Yes,
To hunger and not have, yét hope ón for, to storm and
    strive and
Be at every assault fresh foiled, worse flung, deeper dis-
    appointed,
The turmoil and the torment, it has, I swear, a sweetness,
Keeps a kind of joy in it, a zest, an edge, an ecstasy,
Next after sweet success.   I am not left even this;
I all my being have hacked in half with her neck: one part,

Reason, selfdisposal, choice of better or worse way,
Is corpse now, cannot change; my other self, this soul,
Life's quick, this kínd, this kéen self-feeling,
With dreadful distillation of thoughts sour as blood,
Must all day long taste murder. What do nów then?
    Do? Nay,
Deed-bound I am; one deed treads all down here cramps
    all doing. What do? Not yield,
Not hope, not pray; despair; ay, that: brazen despair out,
Brave all, and take what comes—as here this rabble is come,
Whose bloods I reck no more of, no more rank with hers
Than sewers with sacred oils. Mankind, that mob, comes.
    Come!

    Enter a crowd, among them Teryth, Gwenlo, Beuno.

. . . .

*After Winefred's raising from the dead and the breaking
out of the fountain.*

BEUNO.   O now while skies are blue, now while seas are salt,
    While rushy rains shall fall or brooks shall fleet from
        fountains,
    While sick men shall cast sighs, of sweet health all despairing,
    While blind men's eyes shall thirst after daylight, draughts
        of daylight,
    Or deaf ears shall desire that lipmusic that's lost upon them,
    While cripples are, while lepers, dancers in dismal limb-
        dance,
    Fallers in dreadful frothpits, waterfearers wild,
    Stone, palsy, cancer, cough, lung-wasting, womb-notbearing,
    Rupture, running sores, what more? in brief, in burden,
    As long as men are mortal and God merciful,
    So long to this sweet spot, this leafy lean-over,
    This Dry Dene, now no longer dry nor dumb, but moist
        and musical

With the uproll and the downcarol of day and night
    delivering
Water, which keeps thy name, (for not in róck wrítten,
But in pale water, frail water, wild rash and reeling water,
That will not wear a print, that will not stain a pen,
Thy venerable record, virgin, is recorded).
Here to this holy well shall pilgrimages be,
And not from purple Wales only nor from elmy England,
But from beyond seas, Erin, France and Flanders, every-
    where,
Pilgrims, still pilgrims, móre pílgrims, still more poor pilgrims.
.   .   .   .

What sights shall be when some that swung, wretches, on
    crutches
Their crutches shall cast from them, on heels of air departing,
Or they go rich as roseleaves hence that loathsome cáme
    hither!
Not now to náme even
Those dearer, more divine boons whose haven the heart is.
.   .   .   .

As sure as what is most sure, sure as that spring primroses
Shall new-dapple next year, sure as to-morrow morning,
Amongst come-back-again things, things with a revival,
    things with a recovery,
Thy name . . .
.   .   .   .

59

WHAT shall I do for the land that bred me,
Her homes and fields that folded and fed me?—
Be under her banner and live for her honour:
Under her banner I'll live for her honour.
    CHORUS.   Under her banner live for her honour.

Not the pleasure, the pay, the plunder,
But country and flag, the flag I am under—
There is the shilling that finds me willing
To follow a banner and fight for honour.
    CH.   We follow her banner, we fight for her honour.

Call me England's fame's fond lover,
Her fame to keep, her fame to recover.
Spend me or end me what God shall send me,
But under her banner I live for her honour.
    CH.   Under her banner we march for her honour.

Where is the field I must play the man on?
O welcome there their steel or cannon.
Immortal beauty is death with duty,
If under her banner I fall for her honour.
    CH.   Under her banner we fall for her honour.

60

THE times are nightfall, look, their light grows less;
The times are winter, watch, a world undone:
They waste, they wither worse; they as they run
Or bring more or more blazon man's distress.
And I not help. Nor word now of success:
All is from wreck, here, there, to rescue one—
Work which to see scarce so much as begun
Makes welcome death, does dear forgetfulness.

Or what is else? There is your world within.
There rid the dragons, root out there the sin.
Your will is law in that small commonweal . . .

61

Cheery Beggar

BEYOND Mágdalen and by the Bridge, on a place called
    there the Plain,
    In Summer, in a burst of summertime
    Following falls and falls of rain,
When the air was sweet-and-sour of the flown fineflower of
Those goldnails and their gaylinks that hang along a lime;

   .   .   .   .

    The motion of that man's heart is fine
    Whom want could not make píne, píne
That struggling should not sear him, a gift should cheer
    him
Like that poor pocket of pence, poor pence of mine.

   .   .   .   .

62

DENIS, whose motionable, alert, most vaulting wit
Caps occasion with an intellectual fit.
Yet Arthur is a Bowman : his three-heeled timber 'll hit
The bald and bóld blínking gold when áll 's dóne
Right rooting in the bare butt's wincing navel in the sight
    of the sun.

.   .   .   .

63

THE furl of fresh-leaved dogrose down
His cheeks the forth-and-flaunting sun
Had swarthed about with lion-brown
    Before the Spring was done.

His locks like all a ravel-rope's-end,
    With hempen strands in spray—
Fallow, foam-fallow, hanks—fall'n off their ranks,
    Swung down at a disarray.

Or like a juicy and jostling shock
    Of bluebells sheaved in May
Or wind-long fleeces on the flock
    A day off shearing day.

Then over his turnèd temples—here—
    Was a rose, or, failing that,
Rough-Robin or five-lipped campion clear
    For a beauty-bow to his hat,
And the sunlight sidled, like dewdrops, like dandled
        diamonds
    Through the sieve of the straw of the plait.

.   .   .   .

FRAGMENTS, &c.   83

64

The Woodlark

Teevo cheevo cheevio chee :
O where, what can thát be?
Weedio-weedio : there again!
So tiny a trickle of sóng-strain;
And all round not to be found
For brier, bough, furrow, or gréen ground
Before or behind or far or at hand
Either left either right
Anywhere in the súnlight.
Well, after all! Ah but hark—
' I am the little wóodlark.

. . . .

To-day the sky is two and two
With white strokes and strains of the blue

. . . .

Round a ring, around a ring
And while I sail (must listen) I sing

. . . .

The skylark is my cousin and he
Is known to men more than me

. . . .

    . . . when the cry within
Says Go on then I go on
Till the longing is less and the good gone

But down drop, if it says Stop,
To the all-a-leaf of the tréetop
And after that off the bough

. . . . . .

I ám so véry, O só very glád
That I dó thínk there is not to be had

. . . . . .

The blue wheat-acre is underneath
And the braided ear breaks out of the sheath,
The ear in milk, lush the sash,
And crush-silk poppies aflash,
The blood-gush blade-gash
Flame-rash rudred
Bud shelling or broad-shed
Tatter-tassel-tangled and dingle-a-dangled
Dandy-hung dainty head.

. . . . . .

And down . . . the furrow dry
Sunspurge and oxeye
And lace-leaved lovely
Foam-tuft fumitory

. . . . . .

Through the velvety wind V-winged
To the nest's nook I balance and buoy
With a sweet joy of a sweet joy,
Sweet, of a sweet, of a sweet joy
Of a sweet—a sweet—sweet—joy.'

65

Moonrise

I AWOKE in the Midsummer not to call night, ¦ in the
    white and the walk of the morning :
The moon, dwindled and thinned to the fringe ¦ of a
    finger-nail held to the candle,
Or paring of paradisaïcal fruit, ¦ lovely in waning but
    lustreless,
Stepped from the stool, drew back from the barrow, ¦ of
    dark Maenefa the mountain ;
A cusp still clasped him, a fluke yet fanged him, ¦ en-
    tangled him, not quit utterly.
This was the prized, the desirable sight, ¦ unsought, pre-
    sented so easily,
Parted me leaf and leaf, divided me, ¦ eyelid and eyelid of
    slumber.

66

REPEAT that, repeat,
Cuckoo, bird, and open ear wells, heart-springs, delight-
    fully sweet,
With a ballad, with a ballad, a rebound
Off trundled timber and scoops of the hillside ground,
    hollow hollow hollow ground :
The whole landscape flushes on a sudden at a sound.

67

On a piece of music

How all's to one thing wrought !
The members, how they sit !
O what a tune the thought
Must be that fancied it.

Nor angel insight can
Learn how the heart is hence:
Since all the make of man
Is law's indifference.

What makes the man and what
The man within that makes:
Ask whom he serves or not
Serves and what side he takes.

For good grows wild and wide,
Has shades, is nowhere none;
But right must seek a side,
And choose for chieftain one.

Who built these walls made known
The music of his mind,
Yet here he had but shewn
His ruder-rounded rind.

Not free in this because
His powers seemed free to play:
He swept what scope he was
To sweep and must obey.

Though down his being's bent
Like air he changed in choice,
That was an instrument
Which overvaulted voice.

Therefore this masterhood,
This piece of perfect song,
This fault-not-found-with good,
Is neither right nor wrong.

No more than red and blue,
No more than Re and Mi,
Or sweet the golden glue
That's built for by the bee.

68

'THE child is father to the man.'
How can he be ?   The words are wild.
Suck any sense from that who can :
'The child is father to the man.'
No ; what the poet did write ran,
'The man is father to the child.'
'The child is father to the man ! '
How *can* he be ?   The words are wild.

69

THE shepherd's brow, fronting forked lightning, owns
The horror and the havoc and the glory
Of it. Angels fall, they are towers, from heaven—a story
Of just, majestical, and giant groans.
But man—we, scaffold of score brittle bones ;
Who breathe, from groundlong babyhood to hoary
Age gasp ; whose breath is our *memento mori*—
What bass is *our* viol for tragic tones ?
He ! Hand to mouth he lives, and voids with shame ;
And, blazoned in however bold the name,
Man Jack the man is, just ; his mate a hussy.
And I that die these deaths, that feed this flame,
That . . . in smooth spoons spy life's masque mirrored : tame
My tempests there, my fire and fever fussy.

70

To his Watch

MORTAL my mate, bearing my rock-a-heart
Warm beat with cold beat company, shall I
Earlier or you fail at our force, and lie
The ruins of, rifled, once a world of art?
The telling time our task is; time's some part,
Not all, but we were framed to fail and die—
One spell and well that one.   There, ah thereby
Is comfort's carol of all or woe's worst smart.

Field-flown, the departed day no morning brings
Saying 'This was yours' with her, but new one, worse,
And then that last and shortest . . .

71

STRIKE, churl; hurl, cheerless wind, then; heltering hail
May's beauty massacre and wispèd wild clouds grow
Out on the giant air; tell Summer No,
Bid joy back, have at the harvest, keep Hope pale.

72

Epithalamion

HARK, hearer, hear what I do; lend a thought now, make believe
We are leafwhelmed somewhere with the hood
Of some branchy bunchy bushybowered wood,
Southern dene or Lancashire clough or Devon cleave,
That leans along the loins of hills, where a candycoloured, where
    a gluegold-brown
Marbled river, boisterously beautiful, between
Roots and rocks is danced and dandled, all in froth and water-
    blowballs, down.
We are there, when we hear a shout
That the hanging honeysuck, the dogeared hazels in the cover
Makes dither, makes hover
And the riot of a rout
Of, it must be, boys from the town
Bathing: it is summer's sovereign good.

By there comes a listless stranger: beckoned by the noise
He drops towards the river: unseen
Sees the bevy of them, how the boys
With dare and with downdolphinry and bellbright bodies
    huddling out,
Are earthworld, airworld, waterworld thorough hurled, all by
    turn and turn about.

This garland of their gambols flashes in his breast
Into such a sudden zest
Of summertime joys
That he hies to a pool neighbouring; sees it is the best
There; sweetest, freshest, shadowiest;
Fairyland; silk-beech, scrolled ash, packed sycamore, wild
    wychelm, hornbeam fretty overstood
By. Rafts and rafts of flake-leaves light, dealt so, painted on the air,

Hang as still as hawk or hawkmoth, as the stars or as the angels
    there,
Like the thing that never knew the earth, never off roots
Rose.   Here he feasts : lovely all is !   No more : off with—
    down he dings
His bleachèd both and woolwoven wear :
Careless these in coloured wisp
All lie tumbled-to ; then with loop-locks
Forward falling, forehead frowning, lips crisp
Over finger-teasing task, his twiny boots
Fast he opens, last he offwrings
Till walk the world he can with bare his feet
And come where lies a coffer, burly all of blocks
Built of chancequarrièd, selfquainèd rocks
And the water warbles over into, filleted with glassy grassy
    quicksilvery shivès and shoots
And with heavenfallen freshness down from moorland still brims,
Dark or daylight on and on.   Here he will then, here he will
    the fleet
Flinty kindcold element let break across his limbs
Long.   Where we leave him, froliclavish while he looks about
    him, laughs, swims.

Enough now ; since the sacred matter that I mean
I should be wronging longer leaving it to float
Upon this only gambolling and echoing-of-earth note—
What is . . . the delightful dene ?
Wedlock.   What is water ?   Spousal love.

   .   .   .   .
   .   .   .   .

Father, mother, brothers, sisters, friends
Into fairy trees, wild flowers, wood ferns
Rankèd round the bower

   .   .   .   .

73

THEE, God, I come from, to thee go,
All day long I like fountain flow
From thy hand out, swayed about
Mote-like in thy mighty glow.

What I know of thee I bless,
As acknowledging thy stress
On my being and as seeing
Something of thy holiness.

Once I turned from thee and hid,
Bound on what thou hadst forbid;
Sow the wind I would; I sinned:
I repent of what I did.

Bad I am, but yet thy child.
Father, be thou reconciled.
Spare thou me, since I see
With thy might that thou art mild.

I have life before me still
And thy purpose to fulfil;
Yea a debt to pay thee yet:
Help me, sir, and so I will.

But thou bidst, and just thou art,
Me shew mercy from my heart
Towards my brother, every other
Man my mate and counterpart.

.   .   .   .

74

To him who ever thought with love of me
Or ever did for my sake some good deed
I will appear, looking such charity
And kind compassion, at his life's last need
That he will out of hand and heartily
Repent he sinned and all his sins be freed.

EDITOR'S NOTES

PREFACE TO NOTES

AN editor of posthumous work is bounden to give some account of the authority for his text; and it is the purpose of the following notes to satisfy inquiry concerning matters whereof the present editor has the advantage of first-hand or particular knowledge.

The sources are four, and will be distinguished as A, B, D, and H, as here described.

Sources

A is my own collection, a MS. book made up of autographs—by which word I denote poems in the author's handwriting—pasted into it as they were received from him, and also of contemporary copies of other poems. These autographs and copies date from '67 to '89, the year of his death. Additions made by copying after that date are not reckoned or used.

B is a MS. book, into which, in '83, I copied from A certain poems of which the author had kept no copy. He was remiss in making fair copies of his work, and his autograph of *The Deutschland* having been (seemingly) lost, I copied that poem and others from A at his request. After that date he entered more poems in this book as he completed them, and he also made both corrections of copy and emendations of the poems which had been copied into it by me. Thus, if a poem occur in both A and B, then B is the later and, except for overlooked errors of copyist, the better authority. The last entry written by G. M. H. into this book is of the date 1887.

D is a collection of the author's letters to Canon Dixon, the only other friend who ever read his poems, with but few exceptions whether of persons or of poems. These letters are in my keeping; they contain autographs of a few poems with late corrections.

H is the bundle of posthumous papers that came into my hands at the author's death. These were at the time examined, sorted, and indexed; and the more important pieces—of which copies were taken—were inserted into a scrap-book. That collection is the source of a series of his most mature sonnets, and of almost all the unfinished poems and fragments. Among these papers were also some early drafts.

The latest autographs and autographic corrections have been preferred. In the very few instances in which this principle was overruled, as in Nos. 1 and 27, the justi- Method fication will be found in the note to the poem. The finished poems from 1 to 51 are ranged chronologically by the years, but in the section 52–74 a fanciful grouping of the fragments was preferred to the inevitable misrepresentations of conjectural dating. G. M. H. dated his poems from their inception, and however much he revised a poem he would date his recast as his first draft. Thus *Handsome Heart* was written and sent to me in '79; and the recast, which I reject, was not made before '83, while the final corrections may be some years later; and yet his last autograph is dated as the first 'Oxford '79'.

Of the peculiar scheme of prosody invented and developed by the author a full account is out of the question. His own preface together with his description of the Author's metrical scheme of each poem—which is always, prosody wherever it exists, transcribed in the notes—may be a sufficient guide for practical purposes. Moreover, the intention of the rhythm, in places where it might seem doubtful, has been indicated by accents printed over the determining syllables: in the later poems these accents correspond generally with the author's own marks; in the earlier poems they do not, but are trust- Marks worthy translations.

It was at one time the author's practice to use a very elaborate system of marks, all indicating the speech-movement: the auto- graph (in A) of *Harry Ploughman* carries seven different marks, each one defined at the foot. When reading through his letters for the purpose of determining dates, I noted a few sentences on this subject which will justify the method that I have followed in the text. In 1883 he wrote : ' You were right to leave out the marks: they were not consistent for one thing, and are always offensive. Still there must be some. Either I must invent a notation applied throughout as in music or else I must only mark where the reader is likely to mistake, and for the present this is what I shall do.' And again in '85 : ' This is my difficulty, what marks to use and when to use them : they are so much needed and yet so objectionable. About punctuation my mind is clear : I can give a rule for everything I write myself, and Punctua- even for other people, though they might not agree tion with me perhaps.' In this last matter the autographs are rigidly respected, the rare intentional aberration being scrupu- lously noted. And so have I respected his indentation of the verse ; but in the sonnets, while my indentation corresponds, as a rule, with some autograph, I have felt free to consider conveniences, following, however, his growing practice to eschew it altogether.

Apart from questions of taste—and if these poems were to be arraigned for errors of what may be called taste, they might be convicted of occasional affectation in metaphor, as where the hills are ' as a stallion stalwart, very-violet-sweet ', or of some perversion of human feeling, as, for instance, the nostrils' relish of incense ' along the sanctuary side', or ' the Holy Ghost with warm breast and with ah ! bright wings ', these and a few such examples are mostly efforts to force emotion into theological or sectarian channels, as in ' the comfortless unconfessed ' and the unpoetic line ' His mystery must be unstressed stressed ', or, again, the exaggerated Marianism of some pieces, or the naked encounter of sensualism and asceticism which hurts the ' Golden Echo ',—

*Manner-
ism*

Apart, I say, from such faults of taste, which few as they numerically are yet affect my liking and more repel my sympathy than do all the rude shocks of his purely artistic wantonness—apart from these there are definite faults of style which a reader must have courage to face, and must in some measure condone before he can discover the great beauties. For these blemishes in the poet's style are of such quality and magnitude as to deny him even a hearing from those who love a continuous literary decorum and are grown to be intolerant of its absence. And it is well to be clear that there is no pretence to reverse the condemnation of those faults, for which the poet has duly suffered. The extravagances are and will remain what they were. Nor can credit be gained from pointing them out : yet, to put readers at their ease, I will here define them : they may be called Oddity and Obscurity ; and since the first may provoke laughter when a writer is serious (and this poet is always serious), while the latter must prevent him from being understood (and this poet has always something to say), it may be assumed that they were not a part of his intention. Something of what he thought on this subject may be seen in the following extracts from his letters. In Feb. 1879, he wrote : ' All therefore that I think of doing is to keep my verses together in one place—at present I have not even correct copies—, that, if anyone should like, they might be published after my death. And that again is unlikely, as well as remote. . . . No doubt my poetry errs on the side of oddness. I hope in time to have a more balanced and Miltonic style. But as air, melody, is what strikes me most of all in music and design in painting, so design, pattern, or what I am in the habit of calling *inscape* is what I above all

Style

Oddity

aim at in poetry. Now it is the virtue of design, pattern, or inscape to be distinctive and it is the vice of distinctiveness to become queer. This vice I cannot have escaped.' And again two months later : ' Moreover the oddness may make them repulsive at first and yet Lang might have liked them on a second reading. Indeed when, on somebody returning me the *Eurydice*, I opened and read some lines, as one commonly reads whether prose or verse, with the eyes, so to say, only, it struck me aghast with a kind of raw nakedness and unmitigated violence I was unprepared for : but take breath and read it with the ears, as I always wish to be read, and my verse becomes all right.'

As regards Oddity then, it is plain that the poet was himself fully alive to it, but he was not sufficiently aware of his obscurity, and he could not understand why his friends found his sentences so difficult : he would never have believed that, among all the ellipses and liberties of his grammar, the one chief cause is his habitual omission of the relative pronoun; and yet this is so, and the examination of a simple example or two may serve a general purpose :
Obscu-
rity

This grammatical liberty, though it is a common convenience in conversation and has therefore its proper place in good writing, is apt to confuse the parts of speech, and to reduce a normal sequence of words to mere jargon. Writers who carelessly rely on their ellip- tical speech-forms to govern the elaborate sentences of their literary composition little know what a conscious effort of inter- pretation they often impose on their readers. But it was not carelessness in Gerard Hopkins : he had full skill and practice and scholarship in conventional forms, and it is easy to see that he banished these purely constructional syllables from his verse because they took up room which he thought he could not afford them : he needed in his scheme all his space for his poetical words, and he wished those to crowd out every merely gram- matical colourless or toneless element; and so when he had got into the habit of doing without these relative pronouns—though he must, I suppose, have supplied them in his thought,—he abuses the licence beyond precedent, as when he writes (no. 17) ' O Hero savest !' for ' O Hero that savest ! '.
Omission
of rela-
tive pro-
noun

Another example of this (from the 5th stanza of no. 23) will discover another cause of obscurity : the line

' Squander the hell-rook ranks sally to molest him Identical
forms

means ' Scatter the ranks that sally to molest him':
but since the words *squander* and *sally* occupy similar positions

in the two sections of the verse, and are enforced by a similar accentuation, the second verb deprived of its pronoun will follow the first and appear as an imperative ; and there is nothing to prevent its being so taken but the contradiction that it makes in the meaning; whereas the grammar should expose and enforce the meaning, not have to be determined by the meaning. More-over, there is no way of enunciating this line which will avoid the confusion ; because if, knowing that *sally* should not have the same intonation as *squander*, the reader mitigates the accent, and in doing so lessens or obliterates the caesural pause which exposes its accent, then *ranks* becomes a genitive and *sally* a substantive.

Here, then, is another source of the poet's obscurity ; that in aiming at condensation he neglects the need that there is for care in the placing of words that are grammatically ambiguous. English swarms with words that have one identical form for substantive, adjective, and verb; and such a word should never be so placed as to allow of any doubt as to what part of speech it is used for ; because such ambiguity or momentary uncertainty destroys the force of the sentence. Now our author not only neglects this essential propriety but he would seem even to welcome and seek artistic effect in the consequent confusion ; and he will sometimes so arrange such words that a reader looking for a verb may find that he has two or three ambiguous monosyllables from which to select, and must be in doubt as to which promises best to give any meaning that he can welcome ;

Homo-phones and then, after his choice is made, he may be left with some homeless monosyllable still on his hands. Nor is our author apparently sensitive to the irrele-vant suggestions that our numerous homophones cause; and he will provoke further ambiguities or obscurities by straining the meaning of these unfortunate words.

Finally, the rhymes where they are peculiar are often repellent,

Rhymes and so far from adding charm to the verse that they appear as obstacles. This must not blind one from recognizing that Gerard Hopkins, where he is simple and straight-forward in his rhyme is a master of it—there are many instances,— but when he indulges in freaks, his childishness is incredible. His intention in such places is that the verses should be recited as running on without pause, and the rhyme occurring in their midst should be like a phonetic accident, merely satisfying the prescribed form. But his phonetic rhymes are often indefensible on his own principle. The rhyme to *communion* in ' The Bugler ' is hideous, and the suspicion that the poet thought it ingenious is appalling; *eternal,* in ' The Eurydice ', does not correspond with *burn all,* and in ' Felix Randal ' *and some* and *handsome* is as truly an eye-rhyme as the *love* and *prove* which he despised and abjured ;—and it is more distressing, because the old-fashioned conventional eye-rhymes are accepted as such without speech-adaptation, and to many ears are a pleasant relief from the fixed jingle of the perfect rhyme ; whereas his false ear-rhymes ask to have their slight but indispensable differences obliterated in the reading, and thus they expose their defect, which is of a disagreeable and vulgar or even comic quality. He did not escape full criticism and ample ridicule for such things in his lifetime ; and in '83 he wrote : ' Some of my rhymes I regret, but they are past changing, grubs in amber : there are only a few of these ; others are unassailable ; some others again there are which malignity may munch at but the Muses love.'

Now these are bad faults, and, as I said, a reader, if he is to get any enjoyment from the author's genius, must be somewhat tolerant of them ; and they have a real relation to the means whereby the very forcible and original effects of beauty are produced. There is nothing stranger in these poems than the mixture of passages of extreme delicacy and exquisite diction with passages where, in a jungle of rough root-words, emphasis seems to oust euphony ; and both these qualities, emphasis and euphony, appear in their extreme forms.   It was an idiosyncrasy of this student's mind to push everything to its logical extreme, and take pleasure in a paradoxical result ; as may be seen in his prosody where a simple theory seems to be used only as a basis for unexampled liberty. He was flattered when I called him περιττότατος, and saw the humour of it—and one would expect to find in his work the force of emphatic condensation and the magic of melodious expression, both in their extreme forms. Now since those who study style in itself must allow a proper place to the emphatic expression, this experiment, which supplies as novel examples of success as of failure, should be full of interest ; and such interest will promote tolerance.

The fragment, on a piece of music, No. 67, is the draft of what appears to be an attempt to explain how an artist has not free-will in his creation. He works out his own nature instinctively as he happens to be made, and is irresponsible for the result. It is lamentable that Gerard Hopkins died when, to judge by his latest work, he was beginning to concentrate the force of all his luxuriant experiments in rhythm and diction, and castigate his art into a more reserved style. Few will read the terrible posthumous sonnets without such high admiration and respect for his poetical power as must lead them to search out the rare masterly beauties that distinguish his work.

NOTES

PAGE 1. AUTHOR'S PREFACE. This is from B, and must have been written in '83 or not much later. The punctuation has been exactly followed, except that I have added a comma after the word *language* in the last line but one of page 5, where the omission seemed an oversight.

p. 4, l. 19. *rove over.* This expression is used here to denote the running on of the sense and sound of the end of a verse into the beginning of the next; but this meaning is not easily to be found in the word.

The two words *reeve* (pf. *rove,*—which is also a pf. of *rive*—) and *reave* (pf. *reft*) are both used several times by G. M. H., but they are both spelt *reave*. In the present context *rove* and *reaving* occur in his letters, and the spelling *reeve* in 'The Deutschland', xii. 8, is probably due to the copyists.

There is no doubt that G. M. H. had a wrong notion of the meaning of the nautical term *reeve*. No. 39 line 10 (the third passage where *reeve*, spelt *reave*, occurs, and a nautical meaning is required—see the note there—) would be satisfied by *splice* (nautical); and if this notion were influenced by *weave, wove,* that would describe the interweaving of the verses. In the passage referred to in 'The Deutschland' *reeve* is probably intended in its dialectal or common speech significance: see Wright's 'English Dialect Dictionary', where the first sense of the verb given is to bring together the 'gathers' of a dress: and in this sense *reeve* is in common use.

p. 7. EARLY POEMS. Two school prize-poems exist; the date of the first, 'The Escorial', is Easter '60, which is before G. M. H. was sixteen years old. It is in Spenserian stanza: the imperfect copy in another hand has the first 15 stanzas omitting the 9th, and the author has written on it his motto, Βατραχος δέ ποτ' ἀκρίδας ὥς τις ἐρίσδω, with an accompanying gloss to explain his allusions. Though wholly lacking the Byronic flush it looks as if influenced by the historical descriptions in ' Childe Harold ', and might provide a quotation for a tourist's guide to Spain. The history seems competent, and the artistic knowledge precocious. [See p. 126.]

The second prize-poem, 'A Vision of Mermaids', is dated Xmas '62. The autograph of this, which is preserved, is headed by a very elaborate circular pen-and-ink drawing, 6 inches in diameter,—a sunset sea-piece with rocks and formal groups of mermaidens, five or six together, singing as they stand (apparently) half-immersed in the shallows as described

' But most in a half-circle watch'd the sun,' &c.

This poem is in 143 lines of heroics. It betrays the influence of Keats, and when I introduced the author to the public in Miles's book, I quoted from it, thinking it useful to show that his difficult later style was not due to inability to excel in established forms. The poem is altogether above the standard of school-prizes. [It was published in a limited facsimile edition, 1929, and is given here, p. 130.]

After the relics of his school-poems follow the poems written when an undergraduate at Oxford, of which there are four in this book—Nos. 1, 2, 3, and 52, all dating about 1866. Of this period some ten or twelve autograph poems exist, the most successful being religious verses worked in Geo. Herbert's manner, and these, I think, have been printed : there are two sonnets in Italian form and Shakespearian mood (refused by ' Cornhill Magazine ') ; the rest are attempts at lyrical poems, mostly sentimental aspects of death : one of them ' Winter with the Gulf-stream ' was published in ' Once a Week ', and reprinted at least in part in some magazine : the autograph copy is dated Aug. 1871, but G. M. H. told me that he wrote it when he was at school ; whence I guess that he altered it too much to allow of its early dating. [See p. 143.] The following is a specimen of his signature at this date.

1862–1868

Gerard M. Hopkins.

July 24, 1866.

After these last-mentioned poems there is a gap of silence which may be accounted for in his own words from a letter to R. W. D. Oct. 5, '78 : 'What (verses) I had written I burnt before I became a Jesuit (i. e. 1868) and resolved to write no more, as not belonging to my profession, unless it were by the wish of my superiors ; so for seven years I wrote nothing but two or three little presentation pieces which occasion called for. But when in the winter of '75 the *Deutschland* was wrecked in the mouth of the Thames and five Franciscan nuns, exiles from Germany by the Falck Laws, aboard of her were drowned I was affected by the account and happening to say so to my rector he said that he wished some one would write a poem on the subject. On this hint I set to work and, though my hand was out at first, produced one. I had long had haunting my ear the echo of a new rhythm which now I realised on paper. . . . I do not say the idea is altogether new . . . but no one has professedly used it and made it the principle throughout, that I know of. . . . However, I had to mark the stresses . . . and a great many more oddnesses could not but dismay an editor's eye, so that when I offered it to our magazine *The Month* . . . they dared not print it.'

Of the *two or three presentation pieces* here mentioned one is certainly the Marian verses 'Rosa mystica', published in 'The Irish Monthly', May '98, and again in Orby Shipley's 'Carmina Mariana', 2nd series, p. 183 : the autograph exists.

Another is supposed to be the 'Ad Mariam', printed in the 'Stonyhurst Magazine', Feb. '94. This is in five stanzas of eight lines, in direct and competent imitation of Swinburne : no autograph has been found ; and, unless Fr. Hopkins's views of poetic form had been provisionally deranged or suspended, the verses can hardly be attributed to him without some impeachment of his sincerity ; and that being altogether above suspicion, I would not yield to the rather strong presumption which their technical skill supplies in favour of his authorship. It is true that the 'Rosa mystica' is somewhat in the same light lilting manner ; but that was probably common to most of these festal verses, and 'Rosa mystica' is not open to the positive objections of verbal criticism which would reject the 'Ad Mariam'. He never sent me any copy of either of these pieces, as he did of his severer Marian poems

(Nos. 18 and 37), nor mentioned them as productions of his serious Muse. I do not find that in either class of these attempts he met with any appreciation at the time; it was after the publication of Miles's book in 1894 that his co-religionists began to recognize his possible merits, and their enthusiasm has not perhaps been always wise. It is natural that they should, as some of them openly state they do, prefer the poems that I am rejecting to those which I print; but this edition was undertaken in response to a demand that, both in England and America, has gradually grown up from the genuinely poetic interest felt in the poems which I have gradually introduced to the public :—that interest has been no doubt welcomed and accompanied by the applause of his particular religious associates, but since their purpose is alien to mine I regret that I am unable to indulge it; nor can I put aside the overruling objection that G. M. H. would not have wished these 'little presentation pieces' to be set among his more serious artistic work. I do not think that they would please any one who is likely to be pleased with this book. [See pp. 144–7, and note, pp. 155–6.]

1. ST. DOROTHEA. Written when an exhibitioner at Balliol College. Contemporary autograph in A, and another almost identical in H, both undated. Text from A. This poem was afterwards expanded, shedding its relative pronouns, to 48 lines divided among three speakers, 'an Angel, the protonotary Theophilus, (and) a Catechumen': the grace and charm of original lost :—there is an autograph in A and other copies exist. This was the first of the poems that I saw, and G. M. H. wrote it out for me (in 1866?). [See pp. 141, 155.]

2. HEAVEN-HAVEN. Contemporary autograph, on same page with last, in H. Text is from a slightly later autograph undated in A. The different copies vary.

3. HABIT OF PERFECTION. Two autographs in A; the earlier dated Jan. 18, 19, 1866. The second, which is a good deal altered, is apparently of same date as text of No. 2. Text follows this later version. Published in Miles.

4. WRECK OF THE DEUTSCHLAND. Text from B, title from A (see description of B on p. 94). In 'The Spirit of Man' the original first stanza is given from A, and varies; otherwise B was not much corrected. Another transcript, now at St. Aloysius' College, Glasgow, was made by

Rev. F. Bacon after A but before the correction of B.
This was collated for me by the Rev. Father Geoffrey Bliss,
S.J., and gave one true reading. Its variants are distin-
guished by G in the notes to the poem.

The labour spent on this great metrical experiment must
have served to establish the poet's prosody and perhaps
his diction : therefore the poem stands logically as well as
chronologically in the front of his book, like a great dragon
folded in the gate to forbid all entrance, and confident in
his strength from past success. This editor advises the
reader to circumvent him and attack him later in the rear ;
for he was himself shamefully worsted in a brave frontal
assault, the more easily perhaps because both subject and
treatment were distasteful to him. A good method of
approach is to read stanza 16 aloud to a chance company.
To the metrist and rhythmist the poem will be of interest
from the first, and throughout. [In stanza xiv occurs
the first example of a rhyme which depends on running
over to the next line :

leeward/ drew her D.

It is used also in stanza xxxi, twice,

of them/ of the M : Providence/ of it and S,

and in xxxv :

door D/ Reward : and in other poems.]

Stanza iv. l. 7. Father Bliss tells me that the Voel is a
mountain not far from St. Beuno's College in N. Wales,
where the poem was written : and Dr. Henry Bradley that
moel is primarily an adj. meaning *bald* : it becomes
a fem. subst. meaning *bare hill*, and preceded by the
article *y* becomes *voel*, in modern Welsh spelt *foel*. This
accounts for its being written without initial capital, the
word being used generically ; and the meaning, obscured
by *roped*, is that the well is fed by the trickles of water
within the flanks of the mountains.—Both A and B read
planks for *flanks* ; G gives the correction.

St. xi. 5. Two of the required stresses are on *we dream*.

St. xii. 8. *reeve*, see note on Author's Preface, p. 100.

St. xiv. 8. *these*. G has *there* ; but the words between *shock*
and *these* are probably parenthetical.

St. xvi. 3. Landsmen may not observe the wrongness : see
again No. 17, st. ix, and 39, line 10. I would have cor-
rected this if the euphony had not accidentally forbidden
the simplest correction.

St. xvi. 7. *foam-fleece* followed by full stop in A and B, by a comma in G.

St. xix. 3. *hawling* thus spelt in all three.

St. xxi. 2. G omits *the*.

St. xxvi. 5 and 6. The semicolon is autographic correction in B; the stop at *Way* is uncertain in A and B, is a comma in G.

St. xxix. 3. *night* (*sic*).

8. Two of the required stresses are on *Tarpeian*.

St. xxxiv. 8. *shire*. G has *shore*; but *shire* is doubtless right : it is the special favoured landscape visited by the shower.

5. PENMAEN POOL. Early copy in A. Text, title, and punctuation from autograph in B, dated 'Barmouth, Merionethshire. Aug. 1876'. But that autograph writes *leisure* for *pleasure* in first line; *skulls* in stanza 2; and in stanza 8, *month* has a capital initial. Several copies exist, and vary.

St. iii. 2. *Cadair Idris* is written as a note to *Giant's stool*.

St. viii. 4. Several variants. Two good copies read *darksome danksome*; but the early copy in A has *darksome darksome*, which B returns to.

St. ix. 3. A has *But praise it*, and two good copies *But honour it*.

6. 'THE SILVER JUBILEE : in honour of the Most Reverend James first Bishop of Shrewsbury. St. Beuno's, Vale of Clwyd. 1876, I think.' A.—Text and title from autograph in B. It was published with a sermon by Father John Morris, S.J., on the same occasion. Another copy in H.

7. 'GOD'S GRANDEUR. Standard rhythm counterpointed.' Two autographs, Feb. 23, 1877; and March 1877; in A.— Text is from corrections in B. The second version in A has *lightning* for *shining* in line 2, explained in a letter of Jan. 4, '83. B returns to original word.

8. 'THE STARLIGHT NIGHT. Feb. 24, '77.' Autograph in A.— 'Standard rhythm opened and counterpointed. March '77.' A.—Later corrected version 'St. Beuno's, Feb. 77' in B.—Text follows B. The second version in A was published in Miles's book 'Poets and Poetry of the Century'.

9. 'SPRING. (Standard rhythm, opening with sprung leadings) May 1877.' Autograph in A.—Text from corrections in

B, but punctuation from A. Was published in Miles's
book from incomplete correction of A.

10. 'THE LANTERN. (Standard rhythm, with one sprung lead-
ing and one line counterpointed.)' Autograph in A.—
Text, title, and accents in lines 13 and 14, from corrections
in B, where it is called ' companion to No. 26, St. Beuno's
'77'.

11. 'WALKING BY THE SEA. Standard rhythm, in parts sprung
and in others counterpointed, Rhyl, May '77.' A. This
version deleted in B, and the revision given in text written
in with new title.—G. M. H. was not pleased with this
sonnet, and wrote the following explanation of it in a letter
'82 : ' *Rash fresh more* (it is dreadful to explain these
things in cold blood) means a headlong and exciting new
snatch of singing, resumption by the lark of his song,
which by turns he gives over and takes up again all day
long, and this goes on, the sonnet says, through all time,
without ever losing its first freshness, being a thing both
new and old. *Repair* means the same thing, renewal,
resumption. The *skein* and *coil* are the lark's song, which
from his height gives the impression of something falling
to the earth and not vertically quite but tricklingly or
wavingly, something as a skein of silk ribbed by having
been tightly wound on a narrow card or a notched holder
or as twine or fishing-tackle unwinding from a *reel* or *winch*
or as pearls strung on a horsehair : the laps or folds are
the notes or short measures and bars of them. The same
is called a *score* in the musical sense of score and this score
is " writ upon a liquid sky trembling to welcome it ", only
not horizontally. The lark in wild glee *races the reel
round*, paying or dealing out and down the turns of the
skein or *coil* right to the earth *floor*, the ground, where it
lies in a heap, as it were, or rather is all wound off on to
another winch, reel, bobbin or spool in Fancy's eye, by the
moment the bird touches earth and so is ready for a fresh
unwinding at the next flight. *Crisp* means almost *crisped*,
namely with notes.'

12. 'THE WINDHOVER. (Falling paeonic rhythm, sprung and
outriding.)' Two contemporary autographs in A.—Text
and dedication from corrected B, dated St. Beuno's, May
30, 1877 —In a letter June 22, '79 : 'I shall shortly send
you an amended copy of The Windhover : the amendment

only touches a single line, I think, but as that is the best thing I ever wrote I should like you to have it in its best form.'

13. 'PIED BEAUTY. Curtal Sonnet: sprung paeonic rhythm. St. Beuno's, Tremeirchion. Summer '77.' Autograph in A.—B agrees.

14. 'HURRAHING IN HARVEST: Sonnet (sprung and outriding rhythm. Take notice that the outriding feet are not to be confused with dactyls or paeons, though sometimes the line might be scanned either way. The strong syllable in an outriding foot has always a great stress and after the outrider follows a short pause. The paeon is easier and more flowing). Vale of Clwyd, Sept. 1, 1877.' Autograph in A. Text is from corrected B, punctuation of original A. In a letter '78 he wrote: 'The Hurrahing sonnet was the outcome of half an hour of extreme enthusiasm as I walked home alone one day from fishing in the Elwy.' A also notes 'no counterpoint'.

15. 'THE CAGED SKYLARK. (Falling paeonic rhythm, sprung and outriding.)' Autograph in A. Text from corrected B which dates St. Beuno's, 1877. In line 13 B writes *úncúmberèd*.

16. 'IN THE VALLEY OF THE ELWY. (Standard rhythm, sprung and counterpointed.)' Autograph in A. Text is from corrected B, which dates as contemporary with No. 15, adding 'for the companion to this see No. 35'.

17. THE LOSS OF THE EURYDICE. A contemporary copy in A has this note: 'Written in sprung rhythm, the third line has 3 beats, the rest 4. The scanning runs on without break to the end of the stanza, so that each stanza is rather one long line rhymed in passage than four lines with rhymes at the ends.'—B has an autograph of the poem as it came to be corrected ('83 or after), without the above note and dated 'Mount St. Mary, Derbyshire, Apr. '78'.—Text follows B.—The injurious rhymes are partly explained in the old note.

Line 35. *Shorten sail.* The seamanship at fault: but this expression may be glossed by supposing the boatswain to have sounded that call on his whistle.

Line 47. *Cheer's death,* i. e. despair.

Line 53. *It is even seen.* In a letter May 30, '78, he explains: 'You mistake the sense of this as I feared it would

be mistaken. I believed Hare to be a brave and con-
scientious man, what I say is that *even* those who seem
unconscientious will act the right part at a great push. . . .
About *mortholes* I wince a little.'

Line 101. *A starlight-wender*, i. e. The island was so Marian
that the folk supposed the Milky Way was a fingerpost to
guide pilgrims to the shrine of the Virgin at Walsingham.
And one, that is Duns Scotus the champion of the Im-
maculate Conception. See Sonnet No. 20.

Line 105, *Well wept*. Grammar is as in ' Well hit! well
run!' &c. · The meaning ' You do well to weep'.

Line 112. *O Hero savest*. Omission of relative pronoun
at its worst. = *O Hero that savest*. The prayer is in a
mourner's mouth, who prays that Christ will have saved
her hero, and in stanza 29 the grammar triumphs.

18. 'THE MAY MAGNIFICAT. (Sprung rhythm, four stresses
in each line of the first couplet, three in each of the second.
Stonyhurst, May '78.)' Autograph in A.—Text from
later autograph in B. He wrote to me : ' A Maypiece in
which I see little good but the freedom of the rhythm.'
In penult stanza *cuckoo-call* has its hyphen deleted in B,
leaving the words separate.

19. 'BINSEY POPLARS, felled 1879. Oxford, March 1879.' Auto-
graph in A. Text from B, which alters four places. l. 8
weed-winding : an early draft has *weed-wounden*.

20. 'DUNS SCOTUS'S OXFORD. Oxford, March 1879.' Auto-
graph in A. Copy in B agrees but dates 1878.

21. 'HENRY PURCELL. (Alexandrine : six stresses to the line.
Oxford, April 1879.)' Autograph in A with argument as
printed. Copy in B is uncorrected except that it adds the
word *fresh* in last line.

' "Have fair fallen." *Have* is the sing. imperative (or
optative if you like) of the past, a thing possible and
actual both in logic and grammar, but naturally a rare
one. As in the 2nd pers. we say " Have done " or in mak-
ing appointments " Have had your dinner beforehand ",
so one can say in the 3rd pers. not only " Fair fall " of
what is present or future but also " Have fair fallen ",
of what is past. The same thought (which plays a great
part in my own mind and action) is more clearly expressed
in the last stanza but one of the *Eurydice*, where you
remarked it.' Letter to R. B., Feb. 3, '83.

‘ The sestet of the Purcell sonnet is not so clearly worked
out as I could wish. The thought is that as the seabird
opening his wings with a whiff of wind in your face means
the whirr of the motion, but also unaware gives you a
whiff of knowledge about his plumage, the marking of
which stamps his species, that he does not mean, so
Purcell, seemingly intent only on the thought or feeling he
is to express or call out, incidentally lets you remark the
individualising marks of his own genius.

‘ *Sake* is a word I find it convenient to use . . . it is the
sake of “for the sake of”, *forsake, namesake, keepsake*.
I mean by it the being a thing has outside itself, as a voice
by its echo, a face by its reflection, a body by its shadow,
a man by his name, fame, or memory, *and also* that in
the thing by virtue of which especially it has this being
abroad, and that is something distinctive, marked, speci-
fically or individually speaking, as for a voice and echo
clearness; for a reflected image light, brightness; for
a shadow-casting body bulk; for a man genius, great
achievements, amiability, and so on. In this case it is, as
the sonnet says, distinctive quality in genius. . . . By
moonmarks I mean crescent-shaped markings on the quill-
feathers, either in the colouring of the feather or made by
the overlapping of one on another.’ Letter to R. B.,
May 26, ’79.

22. ‘PEACE: Oxford, 1879.’ Autograph in B, where a comma
after *daunting* is due to following a deletion. *To ’own
my heart = to my own heart. Reaving Peace*, i. e. when
he reaves or takes Peace away, as No. 35, l. 12. An early
draft dated Oct. 2, ’79, has *taking* for *reaving*.

23. ‘THE BUGLER’S FIRST COMMUNION. (Sprung rhythm,
overrove, an outride between the 3rd and 4th foot of the
4th line in each stanza.) Oxford, July 27, (?) 1879.’ A.—
My copy of this in B shows three emendations. First
draft exists in H. Text is A with the corrections from B.
At nine lines from end, *Though this*, A has *Now this*,
and *Now* is deliberately preferred in H.—B has some un-
corrected miscopyings of A. *O for, now, charms* of A is
already a correction in H. I should like a comma at end
of first line of 5th stanza and an interjection-mark at
end of that stanza.

24. ‘MORNING MIDDAY AND EVENING SACRIFICE. Oxford,
Aug. ’79.’ Autograph in A. The first stanza reproduced

after p. 70.   Copied by me into B, where it received correction.   Text follows B except in lines 19 and 20, where the correction reads *What Death half lifts the latch of*, *What hell hopes soon the snatch of*.   And punctuation is not all followed : original has comma after the second *this* in lines 5 and 6.   On June 30, '86, G.M. H. wrote to Canon Dixon, who wished to print the first stanza alone in some anthology, and made *ad hoc* alterations which I do not follow.   The original 17th line was *Silk-ashed but core not cooling*, and was altered because of its obscurity.   ' I meant (he wrote) to compare grey hairs to the flakes of silky ash which may be seen round wood embers . . . and covering a core of heat. . . .   *Your offering, with despatch, of* is said like "your ticket", "your reasons", "your money or your life..." It is : "Come, your offer of all this (the matured mind), and without delay either ! " '

25. ' ANDROMEDA.   Oxford, Aug. 12, '79.'   A—which B corrects in two places only.   Text rejects the first, in line 4 *dragon* for *dragon's* : but follows B in line 10, where A had *Air, pillowy air*.   There is no comma at *barebill* in any MS., but a gap and sort of caesural mark in A.   In a letter Aug. 14. '79, G. M. H. writes : ' I enclose a sonnet on which I invite minute criticism.   I endeavoured in it at a more Miltonic plainness and severity than I have anywhere else.   I cannot say it has turned out severe, still less plain, but it seems almost free from quaintness and in aiming at one excellence I may have hit another.'

26.   ' THE CANDLE INDOORS.   (Common rhythm, counterpointed.)   Oxford, '79.'   A.   Text takes corrections of B, which adds ' companion to No. 10.'   A has in line 2 *With a yellowy*, and 5 *At that*.

27.   ' THE HANDSOME HEART.   (Common rhythm counterpointed.)   Oxford, '79.'   A₁.—In Aug. of the same year he wrote that he was surprised at my liking it, and in deference to my criticism sent a revise, A₂.—Subsequently he recast the sonnet mostly in the longer 6-stress lines, and wrote that into B.—In that final version the charm and freshness have disappeared : and his emendation in evading the clash of *ply* and *reply* is awkward ; also the fourteen lines now contain seven *whats*.   I have therefore taken A₁ for the text, and have ventured, in line 8, to restore *how to*, in the place of *what*, from the original

version which exists in H. In ' The Spirit of Man ' I gave
a mixture of A_1 and A_2. In line 5 the word *soul* is in
H and A_1 : but A_2 and B have *heart*. *Father* in second
line was the Rev. Father Gerard himself. He tells the
whole story in a letter to me.

28. 'AT A WEDDING. (Sprung rhythm.) Bedford, Lancashire,
Oct. 21. '79.' A. Autograph uncorrected in B, but title
changed to that in text.

29. 'FELIX RANDAL. (Sonnet : sprung and outriding rhythm ;
six-foot lines.) Liverpool, Apr. 28, '80.' A. Text from
A with the two corrections of B. The comma in line 5
after *impatient* is omitted in copy in B.

30. 'BROTHERS. (Sprung rhythm ; three feet to the line ; lines
free-ended and not overrove ; and reversed or counter-
pointed rhythm allowed in the first foot.) Hampstead,
Aug. 1880.' Five various drafts exist. A_1 and A_2 both of
Aug. '80. B was copied by me from A_1, and author's
emendations of it overlook those in A_2. Text therefore is
from A_2 except that the first seven lines, being rewritten
in margin afresh (and confirmed in letter of Ap. '81 to
Canon Dixon), as also corrections in lines 15–18, these are
taken. But the B corrections of lines 22, 23, almost
certainly imply forgetfulness of A_2. In last line B has
correction *Dearly thou canst be kind*; but the intention
of *I'll cry* was original, and has four MSS. in its favour.

31. 'SPRING AND FALL. (Sprung rhythm.) Lydiate, Lan-
cashire, Sept. 7, 1880.' A. Text and title from B,
which corrects four lines, and misdates '81. There is also
a copy in D, Jan. '81, and see again Apr. 6, '81. In line 2
the last word is *unleafing* in most of the MSS. An
attempt to amend the second rhyme was unsuccessful.

32. 'SPELT FROM SIBYL'S LEAVES. (Sonnet : sprung rhythm :
a rest of one stress in the first line.)' Autograph in A—
another later in B, which is taken for text. Date unre-
corded. Lines 5, 6, *astray* thus divided to show the
rhyme.—6. *throughther*, an adj., now confined to dialect.
It is the speech form of *through-other*, in which shape it
eludes pursuit in the Oxford dictionary. Dr. Murray
compares Ger. *durch einander*. Mr. Craigie tells me that
the classical quotation for it is from Burns's ' Halloween ',
st. 5, *They roar an' cry a' throughther*.—line 8. *With*,
i. e. I suppose, *with your warning that*, &c. : the heart
is speaking.—9. *beak-leaved* is not hyphened in MS.—

11. *part, pen, pack*, imperatives of the verbs, in the sense of sorting ' the sheep from the goats '.—12. A has *wrong right*, but the correction to *right wrong* in B is intentional.—14. *sheathe-* in both MSS., but I can only make sense of *sheath-*, i. e. 'sheathless and shelterless'. The accents in this poem are a selection from A and B.

33. 'INVERSNAID. Sept. 28, 1881.' Autograph in H. I have found no other trace of this poem.

34. *As kingfishers.* Text from undated autograph in H, a draft with corrections and variants. In lines 3 and 4 *hung* and *to fling out broad* are corrections in same later pencilling as line 5, which occurs only thus with them. In sestet the first three lines have alternatives of regular rhythm, thus :

> Then I say more : the just man justices;
> Keeps grace and that keeps all his goings graces;
> In God's eye acts, &c.

Of these lines, in 9 and 10 the version given in text is later than the regular lines just quoted, and probably preferred : in l. 11 the alternatives apparently of same date.

35. 'RIBBLESDALE. Stonyhurst, 1882.' Autograph in A. Text from later autograph in B, which adds ' companion to No. 10' (= 16). There is a third autograph in D, June '83 with different punctuation which gives the comma between *to* and *with* in line 3. The dash after *man* is from A and D, both of which quote ' Nam expectatio creaturae ', &c. from Romans viii. 19. In the letter to R. W. D. he writes : ' *Louched* is a coinage of mine, and is to mean much the same as slouched, slouching, and I mean *throng* for an adjective as we use it in Lancashire '. But *louch* has ample authority, see the 'English Dialect Dictionary '.

36. 'THE LEADEN ECHO AND THE GOLDEN ECHO. Stonyhurst, Oct. 13, '82.' Autograph in A. Copy of this with autograph corrections dated Hampstead '81 (*sic*) in B.—Text takes all B's corrections, but respects punctuation of A, except that I have added the comma after *God* in last line of p. 56. For the drama of Winefred, see among posthumous fragments, No. 58. In Nov. 1882 he wrote to me : ' I am somewhat dismayed about that piece and have laid it aside for a while. I cannot satisfy myself about the first line. You must know that words like *charm* and *enchantment* will not do : the thought is of

beauty as of something that can be physically kept and lost and by physical things only, like keys; then the things must come from the *mundus muliebris*; and thirdly they must not be markedly oldfashioned. You will see that this limits the choice of words very much indeed. However I shall make some changes. *Back* is not pretty, but it gives that feeling of physical constraint which I want.' And in Oct. '86 to R. W. D., 'I never did anything more musical'.

37. 'MARY MOTHER OF DIVINE GRACE COMPARED TO THE AIR WE BREATHE. Stonyhurst, May '83.' Autograph in A.—Text and title from later autograph in B. Taken by Dean Beeching into 'A Book of Christmas Verse' 1895 and thence, incorrectly, by Orby Shipley in 'Carmina Mariana'. Stated in a letter to R. W. D. June 25, '83, to have been written to 'hang up among the verse compositions in the tongues. . . . I did a piece in the same metre as *Blue in the mists all day*.' Note Chaucer's account of the physical properties of the air, 'House of Fame', ii. 256, seq.

38. 'TO WHAT SERVES MORTAL BEAUTY? (Common rhythm highly stressed : sonnet.) Aug. 23, '85.' Autograph in A.—Another autograph in B with a few variants from which A was chosen, the deletion of alternatives incomplete. Thirdly a copy sent to R. W. D., apparently later than A, but with errors of copy. The text given is guided by this version in D, and *needs* in line 9 is substituted there for the *once* in A and B, probably because of *once* in line 6.—Original draft exists in H, on same page with 39 and 40. The following is his signature at this date:

your affectionate friend
Gerard M. Hopkins S.J.
May 29 1885.

39. SOLDIER. 'Clongowes, Aug. 1885.' Autograph in H, with a few corrections which I have taken for lines 6 and 7, of which the first draft runs:

It fancies; it deems; clears the artist after his art;
So feigns it finds as, &c.

The MS. marks the caesural place in ten of the lines: in line 2, between *Both* and *these*. l. 3, at the full stop. l. 6, *fancies*, *feigns*, *deems*, take three stresses. l. 11, after *man*. In line 7 I have added a comma at *smart*. In l. 10 I have substituted *handle* for *reave* of MS.: see note on *reave*, p. 100; and in l. 13, have hyphened *God made flesh*. No title in MS.

40. CARRION COMFORT. Autograph in H, in three versions. 1st, deleted draft. 2nd, a complete version, both on same page with 38 and 39. 3rd, with 41 on another sheet, final (?) revision carried only to end of l. 12 (two detached lines on reverse). Text is this last with last two lines from the 2nd version. Date must be 1885, and this is probably the sonnet 'written in blood', of which he wrote in May of that year.—I have added the title and the hyphen in *heaven-handling*.

41. *No worst*. Autograph in H, on same page as third draft of 40. One undated draft with corrections embodied in the text here.—l. 5, at end are some marks which look like a hyphen and a comma: no title.

42. 'TOM'S GARLAND. Sonnet: common rhythm, but with hurried feet: two codas. Dromore, Sept. '87.' With full title, A.—Another autograph in B is identical. In line 9 there is a strong accent on *I*.—l. 10, the capital initial of *country* is doubtful.—Rhythmical marks omitted. The author's own explanation of this poem may be read in a letter written to me from 'Dublin, Feb. 10, '88: . . . I laughed outright and often, but very sardonically, to think you and the Canon could not construe my last sonnet; that he had to write to you for a crib. It is plain I must go no further on this road: if you and he cannot understand me who will? Yet, declaimed, the strange constructions would be dramatic and effective. Must I interpret it? It means then that, as St. Paul and Plato and Hobbes and everybody says, the commonwealth or well-ordered human society is like one man; a body with many members and each its function; some higher, some

lower, but all honourable, from the honour which belongs
to the whole. The head is the sovereign, who has no
superior but God and from heaven receives his or her
authority : we must then imagine this head as bare (see
St. Paul much on this) and covered, so to say, only with
the sun and stars, of which the crown is a symbol, which
is an ornament but not a covering ; it has an enormous
hat or skullcap, the vault of heaven. The foot is the day-
labourer, and this is armed with hobnail boots, because it
has to wear and be worn by the ground ; which again is
symbolical ; for it is navvies or day-labourers who, on the
great scale or in gangs and millions, mainly trench, tunnel,
blast, and in other ways disfigure, "mammock" the earth
and, on a small scale, singly, and superficially stamp it
with their footprints. And the "garlands" of nails they
wear are therefore the visible badge of the place they fill,
the lowest in the commonwealth. But this place still
shares the common honour, and if it wants one advantage,
glory or public fame, makes up for it by another, ease of
mind, absence of care ; and these things are symbolised
by the gold and the iron garlands. (O, once explained,
how clear it all is !) Therefore the scene of the poem is
laid at evening, when they are giving over work and one
after another pile their picks, with which they earn their
living, and swing off home, knocking sparks out of mother
earth not now by labour and of choice but by the mere
footing, being strongshod and making no hardship of hard-
ness, taking all easy. And so to supper and bed. Here
comes a violent but effective hyperbaton or suspension, in
which the action of the mind mimics that of the labourer—
surveys his lot, low but free from care ; then by a sudden
strong act throws it over the shoulder or tosses it away as
a light matter. The witnessing of which lightheartedness
makes me indignant with the fools of Radical Levellers.
But presently I remember that this is all very well for
those who are in, however low in, the Commonwealth and
share in any way the common weal ; but that the curse of
our times is that many do not share it, that they are out-
casts from it and have neither security nor splendour ;
that they share care with the high and obscurity with the
low, but wealth or comfort with neither. And this state
of things, I say, is the origin of Loafers, Tramps, Corner-
boys, Roughs, Socialists and other pests of society. And
I think that it is a very pregnant sonnet, and in point

of execution very highly wrought, too much so, I am
afraid. ... G. M. H.'

43. 'HARRY PLOUGHMAN. Dromore, Sept. 1887.' Autograph
in A.—Autograph in B has several emendations written
over without deletion of original. Text is B with these
corrections, which are all good.—line 10, *features* is the
verb.—13, *'s* is *his*. I have put a colon at *plough*, in
place of author's full stop, for the convenience of the reader.
—15 = *his lilylocks windlaced.* 'Saxo cere- comminuit
-brum.'—17, *Them. These,* A.—In the last three lines
the grammar intends, 'How his churl's grace governs the
movement of his booted (in bluff hide) feet, as they are
matched in a race with the wet shining furrow overturned
by the share'. G. M. H. thought well of this sonnet and
wrote on Sept. 28, 1887 : 'I have been touching up some
old sonnets you have never seen and have within a few
days done the whole of one, I hope, very good one and
most of another; the one finished is a direct picture of
a ploughman, without afterthought. But when you read
it let me know if there is anything like it in Walt Whit-
man ; as perhaps there may be, and I should be sorry for
that.' And again on Oct. 11, '87 : 'I will enclose the
sonnet on Harry Ploughman, in which burden-lines (they
might be recited by a chorus) are freely used : there is in
this very heavily loaded sprung rhythm a call for their
employment. The rhythm of this sonnet, which is alto-
gether for recital, and not for perusal (as by nature verse
should be), is very highly studied. From much consider-
ing it I can no longer gather any impression of it : perhaps
it will strike you as intolerably violent and artificial.' And
again on Nov. 6, '87 : 'I want Hárry Ploughman to be
a vivid figure before the mind's eye ; if he is not that the
sonnet fails. The difficulties are of syntax no doubt.
Dividing a compound word by a clause sandwiched into it
was a desperate deed, I feel, and I do not feel that it was
an unquestionable success.'

44, 45, 46, 47. These four sonnets (together with No. 56) are
all written undated in a small hand on the two sides of
a half-sheet of common sermon-paper, in the order in which
they are here printed. They probably date back as early
as 1885, and may be all, or some of them, those referred to
in a letter of Sept. 1, 1885 : 'I shall shortly have some
sonnets to send you, five or more. Four of these came

like inspirations unbidden and against my will. And in
the life I lead now, which is one of a continually jaded
and harassed mind, if in any leisure I try to do anything
I make no way—nor with my work, alas! but so it must
be.' I have no certain nor single identification of date.

44. *To seem the stranger.* H, with corrections which my text
embodies.—l. 14, *began*. I have no other explanation
than to suppose an omitted relative pronoun, like *Hero
savest* in No. 17. The sentence would then stand for
'leaves me a lonely (one who only) began'. No title.

45. *I wake and feel.* H, with corrections which text embodies:
no title.

46. PATIENCE. As 45. l. 2, *Patience is*. The initial capital is
mine, and the comma after *ivy* in line 6. No title.

47. *My own heart.* As 45.—l. 6, I have added the comma after
comfortless; that word has the same grammatical value as
dark in the following line. 'I cast for comfort, (which)
I can no more find in my comfortless (world) than a blind
man in his dark world. . . .'—l. 10, MS. accents *let.*—
13 and 14, the text here from a good correction separately
written (as far as *mountains*) on the top margin of No. 56.
There are therefore two writings of *betweenpie*, a strange
word, in which *pie* apparently makes a compound verb
with *between*, meaning 'as the sky seen between dark
mountains is brightly dappled', the grammar such as
intervariegates would make. This word might have
delighted William Barnes, if the verb 'to pie' existed.
It seems not to exist, and to be forbidden by homophonic
absurdities.

48. 'HERACLITEAN FIRE. (Sprung rhythm, with many out-
rides and hurried feet: sonnet with two [*sic*] codas.)
July 26, 1888. Co. Dublin. The last sonnet [this] pro-
visional only.' Autograph in A.—I have found no other
copy nor trace of draft. The title is from A.—line 6, con-
struction obscure. *rutpeel* may be a compound word,
MS. uncertain.— 8, ? omitted relative pronoun. If so=
'the manmarks that treadmire toil foot-fretted in it'. MS.
does not hyphen nor quite join up *foot* with *fretted.*—
12. MS. has no caesural mark.—On Aug. 18, '88, he
wrote: 'I will now go to bed, the more so as I am going to
preach tomorrow and put plainly to a Highland congrega-
tion of MacDonalds, Mackintoshes, Mackillops, and the

rest what I am putting not at all so plainly to the rest of the world, or rather to you and Canon Dixon, in a sonnet in sprung rhythm with two codas.' And again on Sept. 25, '88: 'Lately I sent you a sonnet on the Heraclitean Fire, in which a great deal of early Greek philosophical thought was distilled; but the liquor of the distillation did not taste very greek, did it? The effect of studying masterpieces is to make me admire and do otherwise. So it must be on every original artist to some degree, on me to a marked degree. Perhaps then more reading would only *refine my singularity*, which is not what you want.' Note, that the sonnet has three codas, not two.

49. ALFONSUS. Text from autograph with title and 'upon the first falling of his feast after his canonisation' in B. An autograph in A. sent Oct. 3 from Dublin asking for immediate criticism, because the sonnet had to go to Majorca. 'I ask your opinion of a sonnet written to order on the occasion of the first feast since his canonisation proper of St. Alphonsus Rodriguez, a laybrother of our Order, who for 40 years acted as hall porter to the College of Palma in Majorca; he was, it is believed, much favoured by God with heavenly light and much persecuted by evil spirits. The sonnet (I say it snorting) aims at being intelligible.' And on Oct. 9, '88, 'I am obliged for your criticisms, "contents of which noted", indeed acted on. I have improved the sestet. . . . (He defends 'hew') . . . at any rate whatever is markedly featured in stone or what is like stone is most naturally said to be hewn, and to *shape*, itself, means in old English to hew and the Hebrew *bara* to create, even, properly means to hew. But life and living things are not naturally said to be hewn: they grow, and their growth is by trickling increment. . . . The (first) line now stands " Glory is a flame off exploit, so we say ".'

50. 'JUSTUS ES, &c. Jer. xii, 1 (for title), March 17, '89.' Autograph in A.—Similar autograph in B, which reads line 9, *Sir, life on thy great cause.* Text from A, which seems the later, being written in the peculiar faint ink of the corrections in B, and embodying them.—Early drafts in H.

51. 'To R. B. April 22, '89.' Autograph in A. This, the last poem sent to me, came on April 29.—No other copy, but the working drafts in H.—In line 6 the word *moulds* was substituted by me for *combs* of original, when the sonnet

was published by Miles; and I leave it, having no doubt that G. M. H. would have made some such alteration.

52. 'SUMMA.' This poem had, I believe, the ambitious design which its title suggests. What was done of it was destroyed, with other things, when he joined the Jesuits. My copy is a contemporary autograph of 16 lines, written when he is still an undergraduate; I give the first four. A.

53. *What being*. Two scraps in H. I take the apparently later one, and have inserted the comma in line 3.

54. 'ON THE PORTRAIT, &c. Monastereven, Co. Kildare, Christmas, '86.' Autograph with full title, no corrections, in A. Early drafts in H.

55. *The sea took pity*. Undated pencil scrap in H.

56. ASHBOUGHS (my title). In H in two versions; first as a curtal sonnet (like 13 and 22) on same sheet with the four sonnets 44–47, and preceding them: second, an apparently later version in the same metre on a page by itself; with expanded variation from seventh line, making thirteen lines for eleven. I print the whole of this second MS., and have put brackets to show what I think would make the best version of the poem: for if the bracketed words were omitted the original curtal sonnet form would be preserved and carry the good corrections.—The uncomfortable *eye* in the added portion was perhaps to be worked as a vocative referring to first line (?).

57. *Hope holds*. In H, a torn undated scrap which carries a vivid splotch of local colour.—line 4, a variant has *A growing burnish brighter than*.

58. ST. WINEFRED. G. M. H. began a tragedy on St. Winefred Oct. '79, for which he subsequently wrote the chorus, No. 36, above. He was at it again in 1881, and had mentioned the play in his letters, and when, some years later, I determined to write my *Feast of Bacchus* in six-stressed verse, I sent him a sample of it, and asked him to let me see what he had made of the measure. The MS. which he sent me, April 1, 1885, was copied, and that copy is the text in this book, from A, the original not being discoverable. It may therefore contain copyist's errors. Twenty years later, when I was writing my *Demeter* for the lady-students at Somerville College, I remembered the first line of Caradoc's soliloquy, and made some use of it. On the other hand the broken line *I have*

read her eyes in my 1st part of *Nero* is proved by date to be a coincidence, and not a reminiscence.—Caradoc was to 'die impenitent, struck by the finger of God'.

59. *What shall I do.* Sent me in a letter with his own melody and a note on the poem. 'This is not final of course. Perhaps the name of England is too exclusive.' Date Clongowes, Aug. 1885. A.

60. *The times are nightfall.* Revised and corrected draft in H. The first two lines are corrected from the original opening in old syllabic verse :

The times are nightfall and the light grows less ;
The times are winter and a world undone ;

61. 'CHEERY BEGGAR.' Undated draft with much correction, in H. Text is the outcome.

62 and 63. These are my interpretation of the intention of some unfinished disordered verses on a sheet of paper in H. In 63, line 1, *furl* is I think unmistakable : an apparently rejected earlier version had *Soft childhood's carmine dew-drift down.*

64. 'THE WOODLARK.' Draft on one sheet of small notepaper in H. Fragments in some disorder : the arrangement of them in the text satisfies me. The word *sheath* is printed for *sheaf* of MS., and *sheaf* recurs in corrections. Dating of July 5, '76.

65. 'MOONRISE. June 19, 1876.' H. Note at foot shows intention to rewrite with one stress more in the second half of each line, and the first is thus rewritten 'in the white of the dusk, in the walk of the morning'.

66. CUCKOO. From a scrap in H without date or title.

67. Autograph in H.

68. *The child is father.* From a newspaper cutting with another very poor comic triolet sent me by G. M. H. They are signed BRAN. His comic attempts were not generally so successful as this is.

69. *The shepherd's brow.* In H. Various consecutive full drafts on the same sheet as 51, and date April 3, '89. The text is what seems to be the latest draft : it has no corrections. Thus its date is between 50 and 51. It might be argued that this sonnet has the same right to be recognised as a finished poem with the sonnets 44–47, but

those had several years' recognition whereas this must have been thrown off one day in a cynical mood, which he could not have wished permanently to intrude among his last serious poems.

70. ' TO HIS WATCH.' H. On a sheet by itself; apparently a fair copy with corrections embodied in this text, except that the original 8th line, which is not deleted, is preferred to the alternative suggestion, *Is sweetest comfort's carol or worst woe's smart.*

71. *Strike, churl.* H, on same page with a draft of part of No. 45.—l. 4, *Have at* is a correction for *aim at.*—This scrap is some evidence for the earlier dating of the four sonnets.

72. ' EPITHALAMION.' Four sides of pencilled rough sketches, and five sides of quarto first draft, on ' Royal University of Ireland' candidates paper, as if G. M. H. had written it while supervising an examination. Fragments in disorder with erasures and corrections; undated. H.—The text, which omits only two disconnected lines, is my arrangement of the fragments, and embodies the latest corrections. It was to have been an Ode on the occasion of his brother's marriage, which fixes the date as 1888. It is mentioned in a letter of May 25, whence the title comes.—I have printed *dene* for *dean* (in two places). In l. 9 of poem *cover* = *covert*, which should be in text, as G. M. H. never spelt phonetically.—l. 11, *of* may be *at*, MS. uncertain.— page 90, line 16, *shoots* is, I think, a noun.

73. *Thee, God, I come from.* Unfinished draft in H. Undated, probably '85, on same sheet with first draft of No. 38.— l. 2, *day long.* MS. as two words with accent on *day.*— l. 17, above the words *before me* the words *left with me* are written as alternative, but text is not deleted. All the rest of this hymn is without question. In l. 19, *Yea* is right. After the verses printed in text there is some versified *credo* intended to form part of the complete poem; thus:

> Jesus Christ sacrificed
> On the cross. . . .
> Moulded, he, in maiden's womb,
> Lived and died and from the tomb
> Rose in power and is our
> Judge that comes to deal our doom.

74. *To him who.* Text is an underlined version among working drafts in H.—line 6, *freed* = got rid of, banished. This sense of the word is obsolete; it occurs twice in Shakespeare, cp. *Cymb.* III. vi. 79, 'He wrings at some distress . . . would I could free 't !'.

APPENDIX

75
Spring and Death

I HAD a dream.   A wondrous thing:
It seem'd an evening in the Spring:
—A little sickness in the air
From too much fragrance everywhere:—
As I walk'd a stilly wood,
Sudden, Death before me stood:
In a hollow lush and damp,
He seem'd a dismal mirky stamp
On the flowers that were seen
His charnelhouse-grate ribs between,
And with coffin-black he barr'd the green.
'Death,' said I 'what do you here
At this Spring season of the year?'
'I mark the flowers ere the prime
Which I may tell at Autumn-time.'
Ere I had further question made
Death was vanish'd from the glade.
Then I saw that he had bound
Many trees and flowers round
With a subtle web of black,
And that such a sable track,
Lay along the grasses green
From the spot where he had been.

But the Spring-tide pass'd the same;
Summer was as full of flame;
Autumn-time no earlier came.
And the flowers that he had tied,
As I mark'd not always died
Sooner than their mates; and yet
Their fall was fuller of regret:
It seem'd so hard and dismal thing,
Death, to mark them in the Spring.

76

The Escorial

Βάτραχὸς δέ ποτ᾽ ἀκρίδας ὣς τις ἐρισδω

I

THERE is a massy pile above the waste
Amongst Castilian barrens mountain-bound ;
A sombre length of grey ; four towers placed
At corners flank the stretching compass round ;
A pious work with threefold purpose crown'd—
A cloister'd convent first, the proudest home
Of those who strove God's gospel to confound
With barren rigour and a frigid gloom—
Hard by a royal palace and a royal tomb.

2

They tell its story thus ; amidst the heat
Of battle once upon St. Lawrence' day
Philip took oath, while glory or defeat
Hung in the swaying of the fierce melée,
'So I am victor now, I swear to pay
The richest gift St. Lawrence ever bore,
When chiefs and monarchs came their gifts to lay
Upon his altar, and with rarest store
To deck and make most lordly evermore.'

3

For that staunch saint still prais'd his Master's name
While his crack'd flesh lay hissing on the grate ;
Then fail'd the tongue ; the poor collapsing frame,
Hung like a wreck that flames not billows beat—
So, grown fantastic in his piety,
Philip, supposing that the gift most meet,
The sculptured image of such faith would be,
Uprais'd an emblem of that fiery constancy.

4

He rais'd the convent as a monstrous grate;
The cloisters cross'd with equal courts betwixt
Formed bars of stone; beyond in stiffen'd state
The stretching palace lay as handle fix'd.
Then laver'd founts and postur'd stone he mix'd
 —Before the sepulchre there stood a gate,
A faithful guard of inner darkness fix'd—
But open'd twice, in life and death, to state,
To newborn prince, and royal corse inanimate.

5

While from the pulpit in a heretic land
Ranters screamed rank rebellion, this should be
A fortress of true faith and central stand
Whence with the scourge of ready piety
Legates might rush, zeal-rampant, fiery,
＊Upon the stubborn Fleming; and the rod
Of forc'd persuasion issue o'er the free.—
For, where the martyr's bones were thickest trod,
They shrive themselves and cry, 'Good service to
 our God.'

6

No finish'd proof was this of Gothic grace
With flowing tracery engemming rays
Of colour in high casements face to face;
And foliag'd crownals (pointing how the ways
Of art best follow nature) in a maze
Of finish'd diapers, that fills the eye
And scarcely traces where one beauty strays
And melts amidst another; ciel'd on high
With blazon'd groins, and crowned with hues of
 majesty.

7

This was no classic temple order'd round
With massy pillars of the Doric mood
Broad-fluted, nor with shafts acanthus-crown'd,
Pourtray'd along the frieze with Titan's brood
That battled Gods for heaven; brilliant-hued,*
With golden fillets and rich blazonry,
Wherein beneath the cornice, horsemen rode†
With form divine, a fiery chivalry—
Triumph of airy grace and perfect harmony.

8

*Fair relics too the changeful Moor had left
Splendid with phantasies aerial,
Of mazy shape and hue, but now bereft
By conqu'rors rude of honour: and not all
Unmindful of their grace, the Escorial
Arose in gloom, a solemn mockery
Of those gilt webs that languish'd in a fall.
This to remotest ages was to be
The pride of faith, and home of sternest piety.

9

. . . .

10

The rang'd long corridors and cornic'd halls,
And damasqu'd arms and foliag'd carving piled—
With painting gleamed the rich pilaster'd walls—
*There play'd the virgin mother with her Child
In some broad palmy mead, and saintly smiled,
And held a cross of flowers in purple bloom;
†He, where the crownals droop'd, himself reviled
And bleeding saw.—There hung from room to room
The skill of dreamy Claude, and Titian's mellow gloom.

11

There in some ‡ darken'd landscape Paris fair
Stretches the envied fruit with fatal smile
To golden-girdled Cypris;—Ceres there
Raves through Sicilian pastures many a mile;
¶But, hapless youth, Antinous the while
Gazes aslant his shoulder, viewing nigh
Where Phoebus weeps for him whom Zephyr's guile
‖Chang'd to a flower; and there, with placid eye
§Apollo views the smitten Python writhe and die.

.   .   .   .

12

Then through the afternoon the summer beam
Slop'd on the galleries; upon the wall
Rich Titians faded; in the straying gleam
The motes in ceaseless eddy shine and fall
Into the cooling gloom; till slowly all
Dimm'd in the long accumulated dust;
Pendant in formal line from cornice tall
❋Blades of Milan in circles rang'd, grew rust
And silver damasqu'd plates obscured in age's crust.

13

†But from the mountain glens in autumn late
Adown the clattering gullies swept the rain;
The driving storm at hour of vespers beat
Upon the mould'ring terraces amain;
The Altar-tapers flar'd in gusts; in vain
Louder the monks dron'd out Gregorians slow;
Afar in corridors with painèd strain
Doors slamm'd to the blasts continually; more low,
Then pass'd the wind, and sobb'd with mountain-
        echo'd woe.

14

Next morn a peasant from the mountain side
Came midst the drizzle telling how last night
Two mazèd shepherds perished in the tide;
But further down the valley, left and right,
Down-splinter'd rocks crush'd cottages.—Drear
   sight,
An endless round of dead'ning solitude:
Till (fearing ravage worse than in his flight,)
What time the baffled Frank swept back pursu'd
Fell on the palace, and the lust of rabble rude!

15

Since trampled Spain by royal discord torn
Lay bleeding, to Madrid the last they bore,
The choicest remnants thence;—such home forlorn
The monks left long ago: since which no more
Eighth wonder of the earth, in size, in store
And art and beauty: Title now too full—
More wondrous to have borne such hope before
It seems; for grandeur barren left and dull
Than changeful pomp of courts in age more wonderful.

77

A Vision of the Mermaids

ROWING, I reach'd a rock—the sea was low—
Which the tides cover in their overflow,
Marking the spot, when they have gurgled o'er,
With a thin floating veil of water hoar.
A mile astern lay the blue shores away;
And it was at the setting of the day.
   Plum-purple was the west; but spikes of light
Spear'd open lustrous gashes, crimson-white;

(Where the eye fix'd, fled the encrimsoning spot,
And, gathering, floated where the gaze was not;)
And through their parting lids there came and went
Keen glimpses of the inner firmament:
Fair beds they seem'd of water-lily flakes
Clustering entrancingly in beryl lakes:
Anon, across their swimming splendour strook,
An intense line of throbbing blood-light shook
A quivering pennon; then, for eye too keen,
Ebb'd back beneath its snowy lids, unseen.

Now all things rosy turn'd: the west had grown
To an orb'd rose, which, by hot pantings blown
Apart, betwixt ten thousand petall'd lips
By interchange gasp'd splendour and eclipse.
The zenith melted to a rose of air;
The waves were rosy-lipp'd; the crimson glare
Shower'd the cliffs and every fret and spire
With garnet wreaths and blooms of rosy-budded fire.

Then, looking on the waters, I was ware
Of something drifting through delighted air,
—An isle of roses,—and another near;—
And more, on each hand, thicken, and appear
In shoals of bloom; as in unpeopled skies,
Save by two stars, more crowding lights arise,
And planets bud where'er we turn our mazèd eyes.
I gazed unhinder'd: Mermaids six or seven,
Ris'n from the deeps to gaze on sun and heaven,
Cluster'd in troops and halo'd by the light,
Those Cyclads made that thicken'd on my sight.

This was their manner: one translucent crest
Of tremulous film, more subtle than the vest
Of dewy gorse blurr'd with the gossamer fine,
From crown to tail-fin floating, fringed the spine,
Droop'd o'er the brows like Hector's casque, and
    sway'd

In silken undulation, spurr'd and ray'd
With spikèd quills all of intensest hue;
And was as tho' some sapphire molten-blue
Were vein'd and streak'd with dusk-deep lazuli,
Or tender pinks with bloody Tyrian dye.
From their white waists a silver skirt was spread
To mantle o'er the tail, such as is shed
Around the Water-Nymphs in fretted falls,
At red Pompeii on medallion'd walls.
A tinted fin on either shoulder hung:
Their pansy-dark or bronzen locks were strung
With coral, shells, thick-pearlèd cords, whate'er
The abysmal Ocean hoards of strange and rare.
Some trail'd the Nautilus: or on the swell
Tugg'd the boss'd, smooth-lipp'd, giant Strombus-shell.
Some carried the sea-fan; some round the head
With lace of rosy weed were chapleted;
One bound o'er dripping gold a turquoise-gemm'd
Circlet of astral flowerets—diadem'd
Like an Assyrian prince, with buds unsheath'd
From flesh-flowers of the rock; but more were wreath'd
With the dainty-delicate fretted fringe of fingers
Of that jacinthine thing, that, where it lingers
Broiders the nets with fans of amethyst
And silver films, beneath with pearly mist,
The Glaucus cleped; others small braids encluster'd
Of glassy-clear Aeolis, metal-lustred
With growths of myriad feelers, crystalline
To show the crimson streams that inward shine,
Which, lightening o'er the body rosy-pale,
Like shiver'd rubies' dance or sheen of sapphire frail.
    Then saw I sudden from the waters break
Far off a Nereid company, and shake
From wings swan-fledged a wheel of watery light
Flickering with sunny spokes, and left and right

Plunge orb'd in rainbow arcs, and trample and tread
The satin-purfled smooth to foam, and spread
Slim-pointed sea-gull plumes, and droop behind
One scarlet feather trailing to the wind;
Then, like a flock of sea-fowl mounting higher,
Thro' crimson-golden floods pass swallow'd into fire.
    Soon—as when Summer of his sister Spring
Crushes and tears the rare enjewelling,
And boasting ' I have fairer things than these'
Plashes amidst the billowy apple-trees
His lusty hands, in gusts of scented wind
Swirling out bloom till all the air is blind
With rosy foam and pelting blossom and mists
Of driving vermeil-rain; and, as he lists,
The dainty onyx-coronals deflowers,
A glorious wanton;—all the wrecks in showers
Crowd down upon a stream, and, jostling thick
With bubbles bugle-eyed, struggle and stick
On tangled shoals that bar the brook—a crowd
Of filmy globes and rosy floating cloud:
So those Mermaidens crowded to my rock,
And thicken'd, like that drifted bloom, the flock
Sun-flush'd, until it seem'd their father Sea
Had gotten him a wreath of sweet Spring-broidery.
    Careless of me they sported: some would plash
The languent smooth with dimpling drops, and flash
Their filmy tails adown whose length there show'd
An azure ridge; or clouds of violet glow'd
On prankèd scale; or threads of carmine, shot
Thro' silver, gloom'd to a blood-vivid clot.
Some, diving merrily, downward drove, and gleam'd
With arm and fin; the argent bubbles stream'd
Airwards, disturb'd; and the scarce troubled sea
Gurgled, where they had sunk, melodiously.
Others with fingers white would comb among

The drenchèd hair of slabby weeds that swung
Swimming, and languish'd green upon the deep
Down that dank rock o'er which their lush long
    tresses weep.
    But most in a half-circle watch'd the sun;
And a sweet sadness dwelt on everyone;
I knew not why,—but know that sadness dwells
On Mermaids—whether that they ring the knells
Of seamen whelm'd in chasms of the mid-main,
As poets sing; or that it is a pain
To know the dusk depths of the ponderous sea,
The miles profound of solid green, and be
With loath'd cold fishes, far from man—or what;—
I know the sadness but the cause know not.
Then they, thus ranged, 'gan make full plaintively
A piteous Siren sweetness on the sea,
Withouten instrument, or conch, or bell,
Or stretch'd cords tunable on turtle's shell;
Only with utterance of sweet breath they sung
An antique chaunt and in an unknown tongue.
Now melting upward through the sloping scale
Swell'd the sweet strain to a melodious wail;
Now ringing clarion-clear to whence it rose
Slumber'd at last in one sweet, deep, heart-broken close.
    But when the sun had lapsed to Ocean, lo
A stealthy wind crept round seeking to blow,
Linger'd, then raised the washing waves and drench'd
The floating blooms and with tide flowing quench'd
The rosy isles: so that I stole away
And gain'd thro' growing dusk the stirless bay;
White loom'd my rock, the water gurgling o'er,
Whence oft I watch but see those Mermaids now no
    more.
            The End
Christmas 1862.

78

Barnfloor and Winepress

'And he said, if the Lord do not help thee, Whence shall I help thee? Out of the barnfloor, or out of the wine-press?'

2 *Kings* vi. 27.

THOU that on sin's wages starvest,
Behold we have the joy in Harvest:
For us was gathered the first-fruits
For us was lifted from the roots,
Sheaved in cruel bands, bruised sore,
Scourged upon the threshing-floor;
Where the upper mill-stone roof'd His Head,
At morn we found the Heavenly Bread,
 And on a thousand Altars laid,
 Christ our Sacrifice is made.

Those whose dry plot for moisture gapes,
We shout with them that tread the grapes:
For us the Vine was fenced with thorn,
Five ways the precious branches torn;
Terrible fruit was on the tree
In the Acre of Gethsemane;
For us by Calvary's distress
The wine was rackèd from the press;
 Now in our Altar vessels stored
 Is the sweet Vintage of our Lord.

In Joseph's garden they threw by
The riv'n Vine, leafless, lifeless, dry:

On Easter morn the Tree was forth,
In forty days reach'd Heaven from earth,
    Soon the whole world is overspread;
    Ye weary come into the shade.

The field where He has planted us
Shall shake his boughs as Libanus,
When he has sheaved us in His sheaf,
When He has made us bear His leaf.—
    We scarcely call that Banquet food,
    But even our Saviour's and our blood,
    We are so grafted on His Wood.

79
The Nightingale

' FROM nine o'clock till morning light
The copse was never more than grey.
The darkness did not close that night
    But day passed into day.
And soon I saw it shewing new
Beyond the hurst with such a hue
As silken garden-poppies do.

' A crimson East, that bids for rain.
So from the dawn was ill begun
The day that brought my lasting pain
    And put away my sun.
But watching while the colour grew
I only feared the wet for you
Bound for the harbour and your crew.

' I did not mean to sleep, but found
I had slept a little and was chill.
And I could hear the tiniest sound,
 The morning was so still—
The bats' wings lisping as they flew
And water draining through and through
The wood : but not a dove would coo.

' You know you said the nightingale
In all our western shires was rare,
That more he shuns our special dale
 Or never lodges there :
And I had thought so hitherto—
Up till that morning's fall of dew,
And now I wish that it were true.

' For he began at once and shook
My head to hear. He might have strung
A row of ripples in the brook,
 So forcibly he sung,
The mist upon the leaves have strewed,
And danced the balls of dew that stood
In acres all above the wood.

' I thought the air must cut and strain
The windpipe when he sucked his breath
And when he turned it back again
 The music must be death.
With not a thing to make me fear,
A singing bird in morning clear
To me was terrible to hear.

' Yet as he changed his mighty stops
Betweens I heard the water still
All down the stair-way of the copse
 And churning in the mill.

But that sweet sound which I preferred,
Your passing steps, I never heard
For warbling of the warbling bird.'

Thus Frances sighed at home, while Luke
Made headway in the frothy deep.
She listened how the sea-gust shook
   And then lay back to sleep.
While he was washing from on deck
She pillowing low her lily neck
Timed her sad visions with his wreck.

80

Nondum

'*Verily Thou art a God that hidest Thyself.*'

Is. xlv. 15.

GOD, though to Thee our psalm we raise
No answering voice comes from the skies;
To Thee the trembling sinner prays
But no forgiving voice replies;
Our prayer seems lost in desert ways,
Our hymn in the vast silence dies.

We see the glories of the earth
But not the hand that wrought them all:
Night to a myriad worlds gives birth,
Yet like a lighted empty hall
Where stands no host at door or hearth
Vacant creation's lamps appal.

We guess; we clothe Thee, unseen King,
With attributes we deem are meet;
Each in his own imagining
Sets up a shadow in thy seat;
Yet know not how our gifts to bring,
Where seek thee with unsandalled feet.

And still th'unbroken silence broods
While ages and while aeons run,
As erst upon chaotic floods
The Spirit hovered ere the sun
Had called the seasons' changeful moods
And life's first germs from death had won.

And still th'abysses infinite
Surround the peak from which we gaze.
Deep calls to deep and blackest night
Giddies the soul with blinding daze
That dares to cast its searching sight
On being's dread and vacant maze.

And Thou art silent, whilst Thy world
Contends about its many creeds
And hosts confront with flags unfurled
And zeal is flushed and pity bleeds
And truth is heard, with tears impearled,
A moaning voice among the reeds.

My hand upon my lips I lay;
The breast's desponding sob I quell;
I move along life's tomb-decked way
And listen to the passing bell
Summoning men from speechless day
To death's more silent, darker spell.

Oh! till Thou givest that sense beyond,
To show Thee that Thou art, and near,
Let patience with her chastening wand
Dispel the doubt and dry the tear;
And lead me child-like by the hand;
If still in darkness not in fear.

Speak! whisper to my watching heart
One word—as when a mother speaks
Soft, when she sees her infant start,
Till dimpled joy steals o'er its cheeks.
Then, to behold Thee as Thou art,
I'll wait till morn eternal breaks.

81

Easter

BREAK the box and shed the nard;
Stop not now to count the cost;
Hither bring pearl, opal, sard;
Reck not what the poor have lost;
Upon Christ throw all away:
Know ye, this is Easter Day.

Build His church and deck His shrine,
Empty though it be on earth;
Ye have kept your choicest wine—
Let it flow for heavenly mirth;
Pluck the harp and breathe the horn:
Know ye not 'tis Easter morn?

Gather gladness from the skies ;
Take a lesson from the ground ;
Flowers do ope their heavenward eyes
And a Spring-time joy have found ;
Earth throws Winter's robes away,
Decks herself for Easter Day.

Beauty now for ashes wear,
Perfumes for the garb of woe.
Chaplets for dishevelled hair,
Dances for sad footsteps slow ;
Open wide your hearts that they
Let in joy this Easter Day.

Seek God's house in happy throng ;
Crowded let His table be ;
Mingle praises, prayer and song,
Singing to the Trinity.
Henceforth let your souls alway
Make each morn an Easter Day.

82

Lines for a Picture of St. Dorothea

Dorothea and Theophilus

I BEAR a basket lined with grass.
I' am só light' and fair'
Men are amazed to watch me pass
With' the básket I beár,
Which in newly drawn green litter
Carries treats of sweet for bitter.

See my lilies : lilies none,
None in Caesar's garden blow.
Quincés, loók, whén not óne
Is set in any orchard ; no,
Not set because their buds not spring ;
Spring not for world is wintering.

Bút they cáme fróm the soúth,
Where winter-while is all forgot
The dewbell in the mallow's mouth
Is´ it quénchèd or nót ?
In starry, starry shire it grew :
Which´ is it,´ star, or déw ?

That a quince I pose upon ?
O no it is the sizing moon.
Now her mallow-row is gone
In tufts of evening sky.— So soon ?
Sphered so fast, sweet soul ?—We see
Fruit nor flower nor Dorothy.

How to name it, blessed it !
Suiting its grace with *him* or *her* ?
Dorothea—or was your writ
Sérvèd bý méssengér ?
Your parley was not done and there !
You went into the partless air.

It waned into the world of light,
Yet made its market here as well :
My eyes hold yet the rinds and bright
Remainder of a miracle.
O this is bringing ! Tears may swarm
Indeed while such a wonder 's warm.

Ah dip in blood the palmtree pen
And wordy warrants are flawed through.
More will wear this wand and then
The warped world we shall undo.
Proconsul! Is Sapricius near?
I find another Christian here.

83

Winter with the Gulf Stream

THE boughs, the boughs are bare enough
But earth has never felt the snow.
Frost-furred our ivies are and rough

With bills of rime the brambles shew.
The hoarse leaves crawl on hissing ground
Because the sighing wind is low.

But if the rain-blasts be unbound
And from dank feathers wring the drops
The clogged brook runs with choking sound

Kneading the mounded mire that stops
His channel under damming coats
Of foliage fallen in the copse.

A simple passage of weak notes
Is all the winter bird dare try
The bugle moon by daylight floats

So glassy white about the sky,
So like a berg of hyaline,
And pencilled blue so daintily,

I never saw her so divine.
But through black branches, rarely drest
In scarves of silky shot and shine.

The webbed and the watery west
Where yonder crimson fireball sits
Looks laid for feasting and for rest.

I see long reefs of violets
In beryl-covered fens so dim,
A gold-water Pactolus frets

Its brindled wharves and yellow brim,
The waxen colours weep and run,
And slendering to his burning rim

Into the flat blue mist the sun
Drops out and all our day is done.

84

Ad Mariam

WHEN a sister, born for each strong month-brother,
   Spring's one daughter, the sweet child May,
Lies in the breast of the young year-mother
   With light on her face like the waves at play,
Man from the lips of him speaketh and saith,
At the touch of her wandering wondering breath
Warm on his brow: lo! where is another
   Fairer than this one to brighten our day?

We have suffered the sons of Winter in sorrow
  And been in their ruinous reigns oppressed,
And fain in the springtime surcease would borrow
  From all the pain of the past's unrest;
And May has come, hair-bound in flowers,
With eyes that smile through the tears of the hours,
With joy for to-day and hope for to-morrow
  And the promise of Summer within her breast!

And we that joy in this month joy-laden,
  The gladdest thing that our eyes have seen,
O thou, proud mother and much proud maiden—
  Maid yet mother as May hath been—
To thee we tender the beauties all
Of the month by men called virginal.
And, where thou dwellest in deep-groved Aidenn,
  Salute thee, mother, the maid-month's Queen!

For thou, as she, wert the one fair daughter
  That came when a line of kings did cease,
Princes strong for the sword and slaughter,
  That, warring, wasted the land's increase,
And like the storm-months smote the earth
Till a maid in David's house had birth,
That was unto Judah as May and brought her
  A son for King whose name was peace.

Wherefore we love thee, wherefore we sing to thee,
  We, all we, through the length of our days,
The praise of the lips and the hearts of us bring to thee,
  Thee, oh maiden, most worthy of praise;
For lips and hearts they belong to thee
Who to us are as dew to grass and tree,
For the fallen rise and the stricken spring to thee,
  Thee May-hope of our darkened ways!

85

Rosa Mystica

'THE Rose in a mystery'—where is it found?
Is it anything true?   Does it grow upon ground?
It was made of earth's mould, but it went from men's
     eyes,
And its place is a secret, and shut in the skies,
  In the Gardens of God, in the daylight divine
  Find me a place by thee, Mother of mine.

But where was it formerly?   Which is the spot
That was blest in it once, though now it is not?
It is Galilee's growth; it grew at God's will
And broke into bloom upon Nazareth Hill.
  In the Gardens of God, in the daylight divine
  I shall look on thy loveliness, Mother of mine.

What was its season, then?   How long ago?
When was the summer that saw the Bud blow?
Two thousands of years are near upon past
Since its birth, and its bloom, and its breathing its last.
  In the Gardens of God, in the daylight divine
  I shall keep time with thee, Mother of mine.

Tell me the name now, tell me its name:
The heart guesses easily, is it the same?
Mary, the Virgin, well the heart knows,
She is the Mystery, she is that Rose.
  In the Gardens of God, in the daylight divine
  I shall come home to thee, Mother of mine.

Is Mary that Rose, then?   Mary, the Tree?
But the Blossom, the Blossom there, who can it be?
Who can her Rose be?   It could be but One:
Christ Jesus, our Lord—her God and her Son.
   In the Gardens of God, in the daylight divine
   Shew me thy Son, Mother, Mother of mine.

What was the colour of that Blossom bright?
White to begin with, immaculate white.
But what a wild flush on the flakes of it stood,
When the Rose ran in crimsonings down the Cross-
    wood.
   In the Gardens of God, in the daylight divine
   I shall worship the Wounds with thee, Mother of
    mine.

How many leaves had it?   Five they were then,
Five like the senses, and members of men;
Five is the number by nature, but now
They multiply, multiply, who can tell how.
   In the Gardens of God, in the daylight divine
   Make me a leaf in thee, Mother of mine.

Does it smell sweet, too, in that holy place?
Sweet unto God, and the sweetness is grace;
The breath of it bathes the great heaven above,
In grace that is charity, grace that is love.
   To thy breast, to thy rest, to thy glory divine
   Draw me by charity, Mother of mine.

86

[*Margaret Clitheroe*]

GOD'S counsel cólumnar-severe
But chaptered in the chief of bliss
Had always doomed her down to this—
Pressed to death.   He plants the year;
The weighty weeks without hands grow,
Heaved drum on drum; but hands also
Must deal with Margaret Clitheroe.

The very victim would prepare.
Like water soon to be sucked in
Will crisp itself or settle and spin
So she: one sees that here and there
She mends the way she means to go.
The last thing Margaret's fingers sew
Is a shroud for Margaret Clitheroe.

The Christ-ed beauty of her mind
Her mould of features mated well.
She was admired.   The spirit of hell
Being to her virtue clinching-blind
No wonder therefore was not slow
To the bargain of its hate to throw
The body of Margaret Clitheroe.

Great Thecla, the plumed passionflower,
Next Mary mother of maid and nun

.   .   .   .   .   .

And every saint of bloody hour
And breath immortal thronged that show;
Heaven turned its starlight eyes below
To the murder of Margaret Clitheroe.

She was a woman, upright, outright;
Her will was bent at God.   For that
Word went she should be crushed out flat

     .   .   .   .   .   .

Fawning fawning crocodiles
Days and days came round about
With tears to put her candle out;
They wound their winch of wicked smiles
To take her; while their tongues would go
God lighten your dark heart—but no,
Christ lived in Margaret Clitheroe.

She held her hands to, like in prayer;
They had them out and ladd them wide
(Just like Jesus crucified);
They brought their hundredweights to bear.
Jews killed Jesus long ago
God's son; these (they did not know)
God's daughter Margaret Clitheroe.

When she felt the kill-weights crush
She told His name times-over three;
I suffer this she said *for Thee*.
After that in perfect hush
For a quarter of an hour or so
She was with the choke of woe.—
It is over, Margaret Clitheroe.

She caught the crying of those Three,
The Immortals of the eternal ring,
The Utterer, Utterèd, Uttering,
And witness in her place would she.
She not considered whether or no
She pleased the Queen and Council.   So
To the death with Margaret Clitheroe!

Within her womb the child was quick.
Small matter of that then!   Let him smother
And wreck in ruins of his mother.

.   .   .   .

87

On St. Winefred

*besides her miraculous cures
filling a bath and turning a mill*

As wishing all about us sweet,
She brims her bath in cold or heat;
She lends, in aid of work and will,
Her hand from heaven to turn a mill—
Sweet soul! not scorning honest sweat
And favouring virgin freshness yet.

88

O Deus, ego amo te

O God, I love thee, I love thee—
Not out of hope of heaven for me
Nor fearing not to love and be
  In the everlasting burning.
Thou, thou, my Jesus, after me
  Didst reach thine arms out dying,
For my sake sufferedst nails and lance,
Mocked and marrèd countenance,
  Sorrows passing number,
  Sweat and care and cumber,
Yea and death, and this for me,
  And thou couldst see me sinning:
Then I, why should not I love thee,
Jesu, so much in love with me?
Not for heaven's sake; not to be
Out of hell by loving thee;
Not for any gains I see;
But just the way that thou didst me
I do love and I will love thee:
What must I love thee, Lord, for then?
For being my king and God.   Amen.

89

S. Thomae Aquinatis

Rhythmus ad SS. Sacramentum

'*Adoro te supplex, latens deitas*'

GODHEAD here in hiding, whom I do adore
Masked by these bare shadows, shape and nothing more,
See, Lord, at thy service low lies here a heart
Lost, all lost in wonder at the God thou art.

Seeing, touching, tasting are in thee deceived;
How says trusty hearing? that shall be believed;
What God's Son has told me, take for truth I do;
Truth himself speaks truly or there's nothing true.

On the cross thy godhead made no sign to men;
Here thy very manhood steals from human ken:
Both are my confession, both are my belief,
And I pray the prayer of the dying thief.

I am not like Thomas, wounds I cannot see,
But can plainly call thee Lord and God as he:
This faith each day deeper be my holding of,
Daily make me harder hope and dearer love.

O thou our reminder of Christ crucified,
Living Bread the life of us for whom he died,
Lend this life to me then: feed and feast my mind,
There be thou the sweetness man was meant to find.

Bring the tender tale true of the Pelican;
Bathe me, Jesu Lord, in what thy bosom ran—
Blood that but one drop of has the world to win
All the world forgiveness of its world of sin.

Jesu whom I look at shrouded here below,
I beseech thee send me what I thirst for so,
Some day to gaze on thee face to face in light
And be blest for ever with thy glory's sight.

90

Oratio Patris Condren: O Jesu vivens in Maria

Jesu that dost in Mary dwell,
Be in thy servants' hearts as well,
In the spirit of thy holiness,
In the fullness of thy force and stress,
In the very ways that thy life goes,
And virtues that thy pattern shows,
In the sharing of thy mysteries;
And every power in us that is
Against thy power put under feet
In the Holy Ghost the Paraclete
　To the glory of the Father.　Amen.

INDEX OF FIRST LINES

INDEX

INDEX